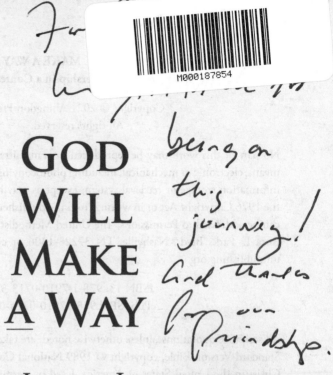

*[Handwritten inscription:]* Fo[r] ... being on this journey! And thanks [fo]r our friendship.

# GOD WILL MAKE A WAY

## SPIRITUAL LIFE *and* LEADERSHIP
### *in a* CONTESTED SEASON

KEN CARTER

*4.21*

Abingdon Press
Nashville

**GOD WILL MAKE A WAY**
**Spiritual Life and Leadership in a Contested Season**

ISBN 13: 978-1-7910-0713-3
ePub ISBN 978-17910-0714-0

All scripture quotations, unless otherwise noted, are taken from the New Revised Standard Version Bible, copyright © 1989 National Council of the Churches of Christ in the United States of America. Used by permission. All rights reserved worldwide. http://nrsvbibles.org/.

Scripture quotation marked *THE MESSAGE* is taken from *THE MESSAGE*, copyright © 1993, 1994, 1995, 1996, 2000, 2001, 2002 by Eugene H. Peterson. Used by permission of NavPress. All rights reserved. Represented by Tyndale House Publishers, Inc.

Scripture quotations marked KJV are from The Authorized (King James) Version. Rights in the Authorized Version in the United Kingdom are vested in the Crown. Reproduced by permission of the Crown's patentee, Cambridge University Press.

21 22 23 24 25 26 27 28 29 30—10 9 8 7 6 5 4 3 2 1
MANUFACTURED IN THE UNITED STATES OF AMERICA

# CONTENTS

# BOOK TWO: WALKING TO THE END OF OUR LIGHT (2018–2019)

# BOOK THREE: GOD WILL MAKE A WAY (2019–2020)

# INTRODUCTION

This is a memoir of a particular season in my life, one that begins with the United Methodist General Conference in Portland, Oregon, in May 2016, and concludes in the approach to a third General Conference in six years. It is my journal and remembrance of relationships, dialogue, ministry, and growth. These are field notes on a journey to a way forward. I had the privilege and task of walking alongside some of the most remarkable people I have encountered in this life. Among them was an astonishing diversity. I have sat with the leaders of Love Prevails and Reconciling Ministries, who tirelessly advocate for the inclusion of LGBTQIA persons in the life of the church, as well as the leaders of the Wesley Covenant Association and Good News, who advocate just as tirelessly for a traditional view of marriage and ordination. I have lectured at Asbury and Claremont, seminaries that largely hold opposite views on much of what divides The UMC. I have traveled across the world to listen to leaders of the church. And I have stood and talked with people who have quietly waited in line to share intensely personal experiences. I was asked with two colleagues to form and moderate a global process with a diverse group of leaders who could discern a way forward beyond the impasse of our denomination. I was asked to serve as president of a global body of bishops. And I was asked to participate in an intense process with a nationally recognized mediator.

At the same time, I was deeply rooted in the local, in Florida, a large and diverse annual conference. We experienced the murders at the Pulse nightclub in Orlando, Hurricane Irma, and the Parkland school shooting in Coral Springs. We began over three hundred Fresh Expressions of church. Over one hundred thousand people worshipped in our churches each week. Our cabinet included active leaders in movements that had very different desired outcomes for our denomination. We had conversations about human sexuality, some precipitated by the Supreme Court's decision of law allowing same-gender marriage in the United States in 2015.

I began this process with a deep desire to help preserve the unity of the church. Along the way that became a more explicit calling to translate a very traditional and orthodox faith into a resource for the full inclusion of the LGBTQIA community in the ministry of the church and the grace of God. For some, the pace of my journey was too quick. For others, it was too slow. Some traditionalists resonated with my theology but not the implications for inclusion that I had sensed. Some progressives could not accept my acceptance and love for traditionalists and respect for their callings.

I want to share something of the journey with you. I have some hesitation, because my life is neither more interesting nor more important than yours. I share this journey, this testimony, for two reasons. I am convinced that what is most personal is most universal. And through the call of the church and the events of history I have been an eyewitness to a people who are trying to make sense of what it means to be a global, democratic, Spirit-led, and inclusive holiness movement.

I listen to people, and I have discovered that if you listen, people will tell you a great deal. These field notes on a way forward are an account of what I have seen with my eyes and touched with my own hands. Thank you for being on this journey with me. The story begins in Portland, Oregon. It commences not with the planned, but with an accident.

*Book One*

# FIELD NOTES *on* *a* WAY FORWARD

2016-2017

# 1

# PORTLAND

In May of 2016, I was attending my first General Conference as a bishop. We had just concluded the opening service of worship and Holy Communion. I had served with Scott Jones, and I can recall that afterward we sat beside each other. Someone came behind us, with a sign. A photographer came in front of us and took a picture of us with a sign in the background. All of this was during the service of worship.

I tried not to become too preoccupied with the inappropriateness of it all.

The service ended, I took off my clergy robe and was walking across the stage when I saw familiar faces, the Florida delegation, seated not far from the front of the hall. *This would be a great time to see them*, I thought. So, I began to walk down the temporary steps that descended from the temporary stage.

As I stepped down I fell, and I quickly realized I could not get up in my own strength. I was surrounded immediately by friends who took me to the nearest emergency room (ER).

In the ER, I was seen by the staff and X-rays were taken. They revealed no broken bones, so the remainder of the afternoon and evening was an exercise in the staff trying to release me and my corresponding inability to stand in my own strength. As the hours went by, they gave me more and more medication, thinking this would mask the pain.

My wife, Pam, finally assured them that I was not a person who was inclined to want to stay in a hospital unless it was absolutely necessary.

Later a staff member asked me, and we were now well into the evening, to lift my leg. I could not.

"Oh," he said. An MRI was scheduled for the next day. And I was wheeled to a room for the night. The MRI, taken the next morning, revealed a ruptured quad tendon. Surgery was scheduled for the next day.

I would remain in that hospital room until the conclusion of the General Conference. I accessed portions of it via my iPad. Friends came by to keep me informed on what was happening. Among them, Robert Schnase stayed an extended time to orient me to the gravity of what was taking place. Other friends came to pray with me. I made very little progress during those days. Finally, I was flown home, to the episcopal residence in central Florida.

There I began the process of physical recovery. The next week I would host an ordination retreat, which was moved to our home. Two weeks later I presided at the annual conference, in Orlando. It would begin immediately following the murders at the Pulse nightclub, which would become a part of its narrative. And a month later I would participate in the Southeastern Jurisdictional Conference, where we would elect five bishops. As with General Conference, this would be my first jurisdictional conference as a bishop. And a week later, I would attend my first meeting of the executive committee of the Council of Bishops. One of their decisions would shape the direction of my calling as a Christian and as a bishop.

# 2

# THERAPY

I began physical therapy, in my home, immediately upon my return to Florida. It would be a process divided into three phases. In the first phase, I had to keep my leg totally straight. It could not bend. This lasted several weeks, and it was to preserve the integrity of the surgery.

In the second phase, I had to begin to bend my leg that had been straightened, to ninety and then one hundred and twenty degrees. This included daily exercises. To bend a leg that had become straight, to be flexible where I had been rigid, was a challenge. Intellectually, it went against what I wanted to do. I wanted to stay where I was.

There was one problem with this way of thinking. This was all happening in June, and I wanted to be able to walk my daughter down the aisle at her wedding in October. I wanted to dance at her wedding, although I am a terrible dancer. So, I was motivated to move, to bend, to become more flexible.

As I did this slow work, a concept came to me: "muscle memory." I needed to teach my muscles to learn again to do the things they had once known how to do. And so, I slowly became more flexible. I began to move.

This also began to take on a spiritual meaning for me. I remembered that our church had once been a movement. We had moved from England to the United States and across the planet. Circuit riders had shared the good news of Jesus Christ. In this movement God used us to spread scriptural holiness and reform the nation.

But over time something had happened. Along the way a movement became an institution. We were no longer flexible; we had become rigid. And in the rigidity we had become harsh and brittle. At times we were harmed. At other times we did harm to each other. A slim book of *Doctrine and Discipline* became a very thick *Book of Discipline*.

In my physical therapy, I worked with a number of women and men. Because this had been a "worker's compensation" injury, I was always assigned to a therapy or a practice. Some were excellent. Others could have done me real harm. I found myself along the way praying that the next medical person I met would be a healing person. And God would invariably send that healing person to me.

I made progress. I was motivated. I was blessed and privileged. I concluded the second phase. I was feeling good about myself, wondering if perhaps I had arrived.

And then the therapist said to me, one afternoon, "You are now ready to move into the next phase. You have regained your range of motion. But you have lost most of the strength in your leg, and now you will need to gain that back."

And so, I began to lift weights. I did not realize how weak I had become. Slowly, and again painfully, I regained the strength in my leg. My goal, by the end of the summer, was to walk around Lake Junaluska. In August my wife, Pam, would take a group to Sager Brown, in Louisiana. I decided to fly to our cabin in the mountains and continue with my therapy there. I had come upon an excellent physical therapist, actually a native of Florida, who was an exceptional teacher. I tried to soak up all I could from him. My insurance coverage would soon run out and I would be on my own.

While there, each day I walked around Lake Junaluska, which is the retreat center of the Southeastern Jurisdiction. It is where my wife and I were ordained deacon and elder. It is where our older daughter was baptized. It is where I attended annual conference for thirty years. And it is where I was elected and consecrated as a bishop.

The walk is about two and a half miles, with a modest upward and downward grade. Each day I made it around the lake. I was deeply grateful.

I gave thanks for the daily physical and spiritual exercises. I gave thanks for therapists and healers. I gave thanks for the gift of being in movement again. I gave thanks for One who had ordered my steps.

I felt strong. And I needed all of this, because I was about to enter into another of the most challenging seasons of my life.

# 3

# WHY WE NEED EVANGELICALS

The word *evangelical* is one of the most abused words in our culture and even in the church. Earlier in my adult life, I almost always encountered this word as we shared testimony or witness, which was grounded in a deeper motivation to reach people outside the fellowship of the church with the good news of the difference that Jesus had made in our lives.

Increasingly, I sense that the word *evangelical* now connotes something very different for many people. I am more likely to encounter this word as I listen to television or radio reports on political elections, or as I overhear conversations about the fragmentation of religious denominations.

So, what does *evangelical* mean?

It is not a synonym for conservative—liberalism has no future without it. It is not a subgroup within a political party or within a church. Whenever *evangelical* is used in this way, something is deeply wrong.

Evangelical is the good news that points to Jesus and his coming kingdom, offering to forgive our sin, overcome our injustices, and heal our divisions. I may have first experienced the good news in a private, personal way. In time, the salvation of God came to include more than my inner world and encompassed my relationships with others and indeed with all of creation For example, the words in Isaiah 1:16, 18, "Wash yourselves; make yourself clean . . . / though your sins are like scarlet, / they shall be like snow," point to personal dimensions of salvation, but they surround the clear calling of Isaiah 1:17 to focus one's attention on others: "seek justice, / rescue the oppressed, / defend the orphan, / plead for the widow."

This was God's agenda, and it was and is comprehensive. If we could achieve all of this, on our own, we would have. The gift granted to an evangelical is that Jesus has done and is doing this for us and through us. The sin of an evangelical is to claim this as an (exclusive) possession within a culture or a portion of the church.

I have been nurtured and fed by the stream of Christianity that flows from the deep reservoir of evangelicalism. I praise God for this gift. And so, I cannot allow such a beautiful, life-giving word—*evangelical*—to be marginalized, scorned, scapegoated, or neglected.

One option would be to simply find another word for *evangelism*. A friend recently suggested *love*. Why not substitute the word *love* for *evangelism*? Here a problem arises: it is also true that in a culture of individualism, we are prone to self-deception. Love may not carry the full weight of God's agenda; it might exclude facets of justice or compassion, courage or empathy or sacrifice. Anyone who has ever experienced betrayal will know that the word *love* carries its own baggage!

The good news—the *euangelion* in Greek—of God's reign was a radical idea that shattered stereotypes and included the excluded. It's crucial that we recover this meaning of the words *evangelism* and *evangelical*— they point to the good news of God's grace in human life. I simply push back a bit against the default notion that we allow the word to be defined by those who fail to appreciate or embody its true meaning. We are in desperate need, in the culture and in the church, of an evangelical movement that does not suffer conformity or captivity to the way it is so often perceived, stereotyped, and yes, even lived.

Why?

Because Jesus was, is and will always be bigger than all of that. This is not bad news. It is good news!

# 4

# ORLANDO

The Florida Conference includes within its boundaries a number of large cities—Miami, Tampa, Jacksonville. We had made arrangements this year to meet in Orlando, in Disney Springs, adjacent to the large theme park.

Early on the Sunday morning preceding our drive over, I began to learn of the horrific mass murders of a number of persons at the Pulse Nightclub in Orlando. A gunman entered the nightclub and opened fire, killing forty-nine people and wounding more than fifty others in what at the time was the deadliest mass shooting in US history. I began to formulate what I would say to our churches that morning and how this would shape our gathering at annual conference.

I began to text Matt Berryman, then the executive director of Reconciling Ministries Network, whom I had known since 2013. He urged me to use the letters LGBTQ in my response, which I did. I wrote a brief word out of that conversation that was shared in many local churches across Florida that morning.

The next day Pam and I drove to Orlando. Because of my injury and rehab I still could not sit in a car. Instead, it was necessary that I lay in the back seat. A local church had loaned us their van, which Pam drove. Pam really was amazing throughout all of this. My physical therapist was not enthusiastic about my presiding at a meeting of over one thousand people. He finally encouraged me to continue to use a walker, even though I was coming to the end of my need for it. "It will protect you," he said. One of our daughters came and stayed through the conference with us, and the other came a week later.

I had invited Bishop Adam Richardson, my colleague, friend, and the episcopal leader of the Florida-Bahamas Conference of the African Methodist Episcopal Church. Almost annually he and I had traveled to the state capital in Tallahassee to pray, learn, and lobby on behalf of nonpartisan bills that benefited the children and youth of Florida—nutrition, civil citations, in-state tuition for students regardless of country of birth.

I had asked Bishop Richardson if I might interview him about the murders at Mother Emmanuel AME Church in Charleston in a 2015 mass shooting, and how he had led his people through that trauma. And in acknowledgment of our full communion, he and I would celebrate in the service of Holy Communion together.

He arrived, along with almost two hundred members from across their church! Of course, the context had now shifted to include the Pulse murders. I framed questions about leadership, compassion, injustice, trauma, prayer, unity, a public and prophetic voice, and he responded beautifully.

The annual conference then affirmed a strong and clear statement about the Pulse murders, with over one thousand persons present and almost no dissent. And then, at the conclusion of a very long day, there was a candlelight vigil.

Because of my stamina, Bob Bushong represented me at the citywide interfaith service. Since he had served strong local churches in Orlando and was the superintendent, this was very appropriate. I had asked Bishops Charlene Kammerer and Bob Fannin if they would preside at particular points along the way, so that I could rest and ice my knee. They were wonderful to serve in this way and since each was a native daughter and son of the conference, the people loved it. One of my favorite memories was sitting with Lucille O'Neal, one of our annual conference speakers and the mother of NBA legend Shaquille O'Neal, and our daughter Abby, herself a former college athlete, and listening to these two tall and beautiful women talk about the challenges and opportunities of buying shoes and dresses!

The conference concluded with the ordination service. I preached and was privileged to lay hands on these women and men. We were only three weeks from having left Portland, and I was coming to the end of my strength, but I had made it through the annual conference. I believed that God had used each speaker, each leader, each act of public witness, and each moment to draw us more fully into the pain and hope of that city and the mission and gift of the church and the gospel in response. I was deeply grateful to God who had been with me every step of the way.

We went back to our room, and I took a long nap. We then loaded up the van and drove back to Lakeland, roughly one hour away. In a season of conferences, the next would be the Southeastern Jurisdictional Conference in slightly over one month's time, where five new bishops would be elected and I would hopefully be reassigned to a new quadrennium in Florida.

# 5

# THE GIFT OF A WHITE STOLE

One of the realizations, once we were back in Florida following all that had happened in Portland, was that my robe and stoles had not made it back. We inquired, but they were nowhere to be found. A friend remarked that somewhere in the world a member of the clergy was wearing a bishop's robe and stole suitable for someone six feet six inches tall!

This did present a dilemma. In a few weeks I would be attending the Southeastern Jurisdictional Conference at Lake Junaluska, where five bishops would be elected. I was inwardly excited that one of our superintendents, Sue Haupert-Johnson, was in a very strong position to be considered. She had been the first clergy elected by our annual conference clergy; she had chaired the order of elders and a General Conference legislative committee; and she was a very effective district superintendent.

The dilemma was that I would need a white stole for this particular occasion. And I was not enthusiastic about purchasing one when I might wear it on very rare occasions. And then it occurred to me that Bevel Jones, my former bishop, would likely not be attending. I had visited him that year at Wesley Woods in Atlanta and his health was failing. We had been close, two native Georgians who found themselves in Western North Carolina. He had the gift of encouragement. And his son, David, and I would often find each other and share a meal at conferences.

So I wrote David: "Could I borrow your dad's stole for the jurisdictional conference?" I gave some of the background and promised that I would return it.

2016  2017  2018  2019  2020

David wrote back the next day.

> Hi Ken. My sister and her husband are living now in Mom
> and Dad's house. She is almost certain that all of his robes
> and episcopal stoles are in a closet in the guest bedroom.
> She will check when she gets home from work and let me
> know. If it is there I would like to give it to you. You were
> one of his guys. And I would like for you to have it and be
> able to use it on occasion if you choose throughout the rest
> of your ministry. It would mean a lot to me to know that in
> that way part of Dad's ministry continued. I will be back in
> touch and if we have it then we can talk about the best way
> for me to get it to you.

Mathew Pinson, a development officer at Emory University and lay
delegate, acted as courier and brought the stole to the conference. I wear it
in honor of one of my own bishops, with great honor, in gratitude for a deep
friendship, and in remembrance of Sue's election as a bishop of the church.

# 6

# My Calling as a Bishop

What was my calling as a bishop? It was internal and external. I was very open to the possibility, but it came from others in a persistent way, their voices, the opportunities, the mentors, men and women, some through affirmation, others through actions. I was given challenges along the way—an $8 million debt in a local church, an economic crisis/meltdown, the deaths of the teenage sons of close friends, denominational board work that created change and shifts in power. In this sense the world of a bishop has been less complex than it might have seemed.

I thought my call was to be a shepherd and teacher and encourager. Most settings are chaotic and the resources are not obvious. I expected it to be so in Florida, and it has been.

But increasingly my calling is also beyond Florida and to the callings of younger clergy, a few laity, the unity of the church, and a better conversation that includes the voices of LGBTQ persons.

Over my life my calling was as a spiritual leader of congregations, but also with clergy (residency in ministry participants, retreats, a couple of grants from the Lilly Endowment that formed cohorts) and a few laity. I struggled to integrate spirituality and administration. It took me a very long time to learn to balance accountability and support.

When I was asked to moderate the Commission on a Way Forward, I found myself in a role that is at the center of denominational discernment around unity and human sexuality. Could I detach from it and truly preside and moderate? Could I see that serving in this way is the best hope for having a better conversation, and, yes, a better outcome?

Had my calling changed? Was it contiguous with this?

I have sought to use restorative justice principles within complaint processes. I have led a service of baptismal renewal when a clergy surrendered his credentials. I have incorporated silence and listening into appointment-making processes. I have shared Holy Communion even when an attempt at a just resolution did not bear fruit.

I wonder—at the end of these four years, of moderating and presiding at the heart of the denomination's decision—will I rediscover some semblance of my initial call?

The joy in this call is creating pathways for others, seeing them and their gifts, and coming to a discernment with them that allows them to flourish.

The work really is discernment for others. And so would be the Way Forward. It is discernment for those who are not seated at the tables where I am privileged to be. In my role, I do not have the luxury of deconstructing the church. I am not a detached consultant, observing, and then moving on.

In the local church I was often advised, when life became difficult, to return to my calling. I have found this to be necessary in the office of bishop as well.

I am in this for people, many of them twenty to thirty years younger than I. In Florida, this has been the Fresh Expressions movement, the Young Adult Missional movement, the M-Lab (design thinking) movement. Within the broader denomination, it would be difficult work of seeking a way forward.

# 7

# THE COMMISSION ON A WAY FORWARD BEGINS

Delegates at the General Conference in May 2016 in Portland had voted to approve the Council of Bishops' request to "pause for prayer" and form a commission to explore options that help maintain and strengthen the unity of the church. There is often a very pronounced critique of study commissions, but the alternative is not to study, simply to meet for a brief time, among people who often do not have shared history or healthy relationships, and whoever has the most power or political skill in building alliances wins in an up-or-down vote.

The result was the Commission on a Way Forward, for which I was asked to serve as a moderator. It would be an imperfect process. The work seemed unnecessary to some and slow to others. The conversations would be in a spirit of vulnerability and trust-building, and therefore would not be public. There would conceivably be thousands of ideas about how it might be done differently. This is not an exaggeration. It is work that I did, not for myself, but primarily for people who are ten to thirty years younger. They are coming into leadership in the church and they will lead well. They deserve every resource and every opportunity. Finally, the commission's work would be in the hands of the larger church. And having said all of this, I was and still am hopeful, because God can do abundantly far more than I can ask or imagine.

Given the authority (by a fairly close margin) to form a commission,

I assumed our first step would be to compose the commission—that is, to name those who would be members of it. However, Cynthia Fierro Harvey noted that we should take a farther step back and identify the mission, vision, and scope of the work. I began to develop a draft of that, and other members of the council shaped and revised it. This is the key sentence:

> The Commission will design a way for being church that maximizes the presence of a United Methodist witness in as many places in the world as possible, that allows for as much contextual differentiation as possible, and that balances an approach to different theological understandings of human sexuality with a desire for as much unity as possible.

I remember that the recurrence of the words *as possible* was grounded in a dose of realism following the 2016 General Conference. We were and are a deeply divided church.

The bishops then nominated and selected thirty-two members to serve on the Commission, focusing on a diverse body that represents our global church. In the commission there were persons from nine countries with a variety of theological perspectives. The commission was one-third laity, one-third clergy, and one-third bishops, and it included younger persons, gay persons, professors, administrators, pastors, youth ministers, campus ministers, lay leaders, large church pastors, and persons identified with renewal and advocacy groups. There was Korean, Hispanic, African-American, Filipino, European, and African representation.

Two key decisions greatly blessed our work. The first was an invitation to Gil Rendle to serve as our consultant. I knew Gil and had great respect for him. At the DS/SCM training in Lake Junaluska in August of 2016, Sandra Steiner Ball and I had breakfast with him. He noted that he was moving toward retirement and had a desire not to spend time in airports.

We did invite him to help us, and then I made two comments. I told him that however he responded within his own sense of call, we would respect him and would remain friends. And secondly, I told him that we would work hard to minimize his time in airports!

In time, Gil agreed to consult with us. He actually worked as a coach to the moderators, and in each meeting he gave a presentation. As the work flowed through the Council of Bishops, Gil was present at those meetings as well.

The other decision was related to the management of the project. When I arrived in Florida, I met a pastor named Alex Shanks who had extraordinary gifts in administration. At the conclusion of my first four years, and upon the retirement of David Dodge, who himself had been excellent in the role of assistant to the bishop, I asked Alex to serve. He was thirty-nine years old and was the lead pastor of one of the fastest growing churches in our denomination (First Church, Coral Springs). It soon became evident that he had real gifts for this work.

It became apparent as well, as we began the work of the commission, that we would need someone with Alex's skills to assist in the implementation of the Way Forward process. Alex was open to this work, and so he was present at every meeting. He was the liaison with GCFA, with the sites where we met, mostly the buildings of our general boards and agencies. He was the link with the work we did at Wespath and with Bill Waddell, legal counsel for the Council of Bishops. The meetings happened flawlessly and came in under budget. Alex gained the respect of every member of the commission, regardless of their position. And, most significantly, he did all of this as a volunteer.

At one point I said to him, it is simply not fair that you are doing this work for no compensation. It is extra work. And he responded, "All of the members of the commission and the moderators are doing this as volunteers. And I am willing to do so as well." Both Alex and Gil were great blessings in the Commission on a Way Forward.

As we began our early work in the commission, our first priority was to build trust and intentional community among a group of people who had good reasons not to trust each other. At the heart of this relationship building was the book *The Anatomy of Peace* by the Arbinger Institute, which focuses on how we live with a heart at war, seeing others as obstacles to or vehicles for what we want, or a heart at peace, seeing others as people.

2016    2017    2018    2019    2020

I had used this resource in coach training with Spiritual Leadership, Inc., as had several other members of the commission—Debbie Wallace Padgett, Sandra Steiner Ball, Jorge Acevedo, and Julie Hager Love.

*The Anatomy of Peace* is rooted in the philosophy of Martin Buber. A heart at war exaggerates our differences. A heart at peace sees what we have in common. The commission wrote a significant covenant with each other, and at the end of the first meeting we gave everyone the invitation to leave, with honor. Commission members focused on finding a way forward rather than on representing groups or constituencies. This was complex, because the group included persons who were in some instances employed by these organizations or in governance positions with them.

The commission's practice of voicing differing theological views and interpretations of Scripture stood and stands as a model for what kind of ministry we are both called and empowered by God to do. This led us to discover the interests behind the various positions, in Gil Rendle's language, and opened up multiple possibilities for how the church could continue to fulfill the ministry of Christ in both unity and with diversity.

The early meetings were some of the most difficult and complex work I have ever done. The moderators consulted with each other each step of the way. Gil was a wise voice. It was not clear what would be possible. But we had begun our work.

# 8

# An Eclectic Spiritual Plan

At the beginning of a calendar year I often share a spiritual plan with the people of the annual conference. As always, they may have their own way of going about spiritual growth, and that is great. I simply believe a plan is better than no plan, and this becomes for me, in Wesley's language, an "ordinary channel" of God's grace. At the beginning of 2017, my spiritual plan was a vital resource in sustaining me through daily, weekly, and monthly patterns, as the Commission on a Way Forward began its work.

I realize I have had an eclectic spiritual journey as a Methodist. I use the *Book of Common Prayer* (rite two) most mornings. At my best I follow a practice of sabbath than I learned from Jewish friends in Greensboro. I often read the *Moravian Daily Texts* and have given this as a Christmas gift for years—I associate it with Pam's home of Kernersville, North Carolina, and the love feast traditions when we were in Winston-Salem. Each day has two verses of Scripture, one from the Old Testament and one from the New Testament. Two hymn texts and a prayer are also included. This was my place to begin. When I had more time, I tried to come back to a word that is in one of the two verses (similar to Centering Prayer) and stay with that word. I am an early morning person, by nature, so I began the day in this way.

The word on January 2, 2017, was "according to your mercy." I tried for several minutes to stay with this phrase. And whenever I would drift to something else, I would return to it. The word for January 3 was "be merciful." Both came from the daily verses in the *MDT*.

I also spend time with the Pendle Hill Pamphlet series from the Quakers. I remember as a kid that my grandfather, who was a conscientious objector and a Quaker, subscribed to them and read them.

None of these resources are particularly Methodist, and yet I think that this is true to John Wesley. He was Anglican in the ordering of his spiritual life. He was influenced by the Moravians in seeking a deep personal faith. He was influenced (to a degree) by the Protestant reformers and the Eastern Fathers.

And yet the gift of being a Methodist, at our best—and we are not always at our best—is seeking to bring all of this together toward some greater purpose. We use the language of the transformation of the world, or on most days the transformation of neighborhoods, or even the transformation of the people who gather inside our churches.

One morning early in 2017 I read Acts 10, one of the lections for Baptism of the Lord Sunday, and I was struck by Peter's preaching that "God shows no partiality." The day before, I had toured the National Civil Rights Museum during a visit to Memphis. It portrays the history of segregation, separation, discrimination, and violence. My Scripture reading reminded me that the problem of racism is heresy. We do not always listen to the voices of apostles and prophets.

Journaling was also part of my spiritual plan in 2017, as it has been for many years. In addition to writing down much of my daily experiences— meeting notes, to-do lists, summaries of conversations, what I need to pack for travel, doodling—I try to write daily reflections on something I have read in the Scriptures, as well as call to mind persons who have asked for prayers.

A complication for me is that I travel a great deal. So how do I travel with these tools to continue my spiritual plan? The *Moravian Daily Texts* is a small book, and while I could access it online, I take the book with me, because I often write in it. I read from a Bible when I am at home and I often take a small NRSV translation of the New Testament and Psalms when I travel. And my journal goes with me wherever I go. All of this could be done on an iPad, of course, but I am not there, technologically. I like to hold a book in my hands and write with a pen in a notebook.

Some time each day, some intellectual growth, some silence, some reflection on what is happening—all of this contributes to our being more available to God and more self-aware of what is happening around us. It is one way—not the only way, but one way—that we become disciples of Jesus Christ for the transformation of the world.

In early 2017, as the Trump administration began and the Commission on a Way Forward's challenging work stood ahead, rereading *The Anatomy of Peace* (Arbinger Institute) reminded me that I needed a heart at peace—a deeply formed spiritual center with the Jesus who walks alongside the most vulnerable in our nation, a deeply formed center that is not a heart at war, not in collusion with those who want to sustain the conflict of the culture wars or the red-blue state divides, or the mirror images of that division in our denomination. I need a heart at peace that will bring about a change in myself, a change that will be attractive enough to draw people away from divisions toward a spiritual center rooted in something like the Sermon the Mount—a change that announces, "He (Jesus) must increase, I must decrease." I need a change that is nonviolent, that does not exaggerate the differences between people, but builds bridges toward them. And, to lean into a Wesleyan direction, I need a change that sees a heart at peace as the compassion that Jesus links with perfection/holiness in Matthew 5:48 and Luke 6:36. My spiritual plan was a vital resource to guide and sustain me, to help me attain and keep a heart at peace throughout this season.

A quiet time with God is essential, and I am an early morning person. But it ought to lead to something—more opportunity, more equality, more flourishing, more patience, more justice, more covenant-keeping, more hope, more and deeper followers of Jesus; and, said differently, less unfairness, less judgmentalism, less prejudice, less violence, less despair, less hunger, less racism, less sexual harassment, less mimicking of unhealthy patterns of behavior that we see in the world.

We aim to be used by God for the transformation of the world. It begins with a fire, a warm heart; but it does not end there. Philosophers would say this is necessary but not sufficient. I love being a Methodist. At its core this is all very simple. It is beginning the day with God. It is knowing that other traditions can help us come into the presence of this God. And then it is knowing that the unfinished business of time with God is the day we will spend in God's world.

# To Clergy Friends after the Election: Some Thoughts

*The end of 2016 saw the election of Donald Trump as president of the United States in an especially divisive election. I wrote the following letter to my UMC clergy colleagues as a way of reflecting on how we might respond.*

People talk to me, and I am blessed by friends who have walked many different paths. I am aware that many clergy are struggling after the recent presidential election, and for different reasons. It may help to name some of this.

1. Some of us felt that America was on a path to the kingdom (reign) of God—more inclusive, more just—and this was symbolized by an African-American president and next a female president. The surprising election results to many were a disruption of this progress. Our mistake was fusing together the nation-state and the church, as if they were one. This can be seen in some of the discussion around the National Cathedral and the National Prayer Breakfast. The call is to repentance—the church was and is always an alternative community. We are not one of the two political parties at prayer.

2. Some of us with more evangelical temperaments have made an uneasy alliance with Trump. In conversation this group tends to shut down or change the subject, but it was and is really untenable to hold together a Christian

evangelical spirit with something like Breitbart. And so
the voices of *Christianity Today* and Asbury Seminary have
been quite clear in their critique of many of the devel-
opments of the new administration. The older binary of
pitting the mainline against evangelicals does not quite
work here. There is and can be a Christian consensus on
much that is ahead (mass incarceration, for example), if
we will seek it. And in the end, one of the great dangers
is that collusion with the alt-right (and white supremacy)
damages the evangelical brand.

3.  Some of us are searching for the common good and the
    core values underneath the partisan divide. There is deep
    wisdom in both our national creeds and in our Scriptures
    about welcoming the stranger. There is the undeniable
    history of wave after wave of immigrants. There is the
    tragic reality of ways we have harmed "the other" in the
    past. To call people back to who we are—and again, if
    we listen this is happening across a wide spectrum—is a
    necessary witness.

4.  Some of us are discouraged in that life becomes
    bifurcated—externally, in our workplace or in our fami-
    lies we present a face that is calm, assured, pleasant; pri-
    vately, among a circle of friends or in a private Facebook
    group, people are honest. Positively, this provides sup-
    port. But negatively, we do not integrate our core convic-
    tions with our professional life.

5.  As worship leaders and preachers, we often live on two
    extremes of a continuum. We either say nothing about
    what is going on, or we do so in a way that is political
    without being theological. To avoid the subject is to miss
    the opportunity to minister to people who are sitting
    in our congregations and wanting to process all of this
    before God. To simply share what we have heard on our

favorite television news network is to offer them less than the gospel. The voices of prophets and the teachings of Jesus surely have something to say about how we love our neighbors and the cost of not doing so in this life and the life to come.

6. Many want the Council of Bishops to speak. Most bishops in the US have spoken. The COB is a global group, on four continents, with many national agendas. It is not a US centric body. What people may want is for the COB to tell others what to do, so that their preferred outcome will somehow come to be. The bishops speak to the churches and not for the churches. Adaptive leadership really is about our taking responsibility in our own contexts to interpret the Word of God for our people. At our best, we simply speak from where we are and give others some language that they can adapt to their own settings.

7. Following the insights of the Franciscan Richard Rohr, we might reflect on the addictive nature of the political conversation at the moment. Is it dualistic? Yes. Does it stereotype? Yes. Is it blaming and judgmental? Yes. Can we detach from it? This may be more difficult. I have come to the conclusion that I may need to watch no more than one hour a day of news. And many have said to me that they have left Facebook and Twitter because it was unhealthy.

8. We are in need of a spirituality of activism. Our nation is in a time of political chaos. As someone has said, when they go low, we must go deeper. The church cannot take on the role of the government in meeting every human need, but we will need to clarify what we are called to do and be when the market economy will increasingly shape health care and education. We can begin by reading and praying the Sermon on the Mount.

9. We will need to avoid all or nothing thinking. Between the individual (who feels powerless) and the national government (which has been demonized in the past and is increasingly now) are a number of mediating institutions—cities, nonprofits, foundations, churches, ministries. Leaders will need to think creatively about the common good and the unfinished work to be done, especially with racism, inequality of opportunity, and xenophobia. And yet there are significant resources across our nation to do this work.

10. We will need to develop a simple, clear, and consistent moral framework. Even if we are increasingly a post-Christian culture, we have (to borrow the language of Rowan Williams) a Christian memory. The parables and teachings of Jesus—the Good Samaritan in Luke 10 or the Great Judgment in Matthew 25—are there to be explored, shared, and lived. We will need to find our voice. The good news, as my preaching professor Richard Lischer once said, is that we have great material.

So do not lose heart. Who knows if God has not called us for such a time as this?

# 9

# A CONVERSATION WITH BISHOP WOODIE WHITE

As the Commission on a Way Forward began its work, questions emerged: What were the implications of a possible restructuring? And how could we learn from our past history of division, segregation, and reunion?

We invited Bishop Woodie White to speak with the commission, and I interviewed him, within our meeting and again just following. I consider him to be one of the living saints and prophets of our movement. Bishop White was the founding General Secretary of the General Commission on Religion and Race; later a bishop of the church in Indiana and Illinois and Bishop in Residence at Emory University. I knew that the Way Forward would need to engage with our complicated and flawed history if we were to have any hope of not repeating past sins and errors.

I asked him what it was like to be a leader as the church united and as it later sought unity after desegregation, to talk about some of the principles that helped the church move through those times and how that might be relevant for us. He reflected, "Well, I think the most important principle is a commitment that the church will hold together. There were people in that time who believed that the church would divide over the issue of racial inclusiveness. But I think for the most part the church said we're going to hold together and try to address all of the issues that seem to divide us and move forward as it were. So that was the basic commitment, that we're going to stay together."

In the area of race, which is an unfinished agenda, Bishop White has been a voice of leadership. Once a year he writes a "birthday letter" to Dr. Martin Luther King Jr., in which he gives a perspective on race relations in the US, and many in our denomination read his letter each year. Given the advances and at times what appear to be setbacks, I asked him to reflect on what sustained him as a leader, as a bishop, and as a Christian.

He responded, "I always see progress. I always see progress. The church does not move as fast as I would like it to move. Sometimes progress is not permanent. But what sustains me and what increases my hope is that I always see the church getting better. It's never what I want it to be, but it's not what it used to be! And I think that if people can see that they won't get discouraged, they won't become cynical, and they won't lose hope, because they can see changes and know there is progress. And so, this is what sustains me."

In his presentation to the Commission on a Way Forward, Bishop White reflected on the Central Jurisdiction as a part of our history in American Methodism. He mentioned Bishop L. Scott Allen, the last bishop to be elected by the Central Jurisdiction; Bishop Allen ordained me, right after I had graduated from divinity school. I asked Bishop White about lessons that could be learned from the Central Jurisdiction for a time such as this.

Again, Bishop White noted, "Changes are never guaranteed, and progress is never guaranteed in terms of permanence. So, you are always having to work at it. You are always having to evaluate. You are always having to address an issue. And if we stay alert and continue to stay on top of our progress, I think we will assure that we will get to where we want to be. But if we ever kind of let our guard down, if we think, wow, we have solved the problem, then we just get the problem reinventing itself! That is what happens."

Lastly, I asked Bishop White what he had learned from a decade with students at Candler as their bishop in residence. He smiled and then responded, "The thing that surprised me was how little sense of history they had. They did not know where the church had been and so they didn't have an appropriate appreciation for the accomplishments of those who had gone before them, an awareness of some of the sacrifices that had been made. And I found myself then in a position to help them understand where the church was and what sacrifices had been made by those who had gone before. And then I was able to say to them that those forebears didn't do all the work! They saved some of that work for you and you have to pick it up!"

# CHARLOTTESVILLE

*In August 2017, violence broke out in Charlottesville, Virginia, during a white supremacist rally protesting the removal of a statue of confederate general Robert E. Lee.*

L ast Saturday, I began to learn of the events of Charlottesville. I stated that, as a follower of Jesus and a graduate of the University of Virginia, I found this repulsive. Later that evening, knowing that many would worship in local churches the next morning, I invited us to lay our racism at the altar and ask God to remove it from us.

On Tuesday, the Southeastern Jurisdiction College of Bishops of The United Methodist Church met in Atlanta. Bishop Sharma D. Lewis, the resident bishop of Virginia, led us in a devotional on the last few days in #Charlottesville. She described her ministry in response to these events, calling the people of her area to prayer, action, and continuing dialogue. She has ministered to the surviving spouse of one of those who died, who is a United Methodist. She asked us to name our feelings about the events of the weekend: I used one of the words I wrote on Saturday, that it was *repulsive*. I also mentioned words like *sadness, heavy, tired, privileged,* and *troubled.*

She then asked us to invite Jesus into the conversation. What would he say? I heard these words from the Lord: "I will not leave you comfortless" (John 14:18 KJV). I thought of the processional of hatred on the lawn of the University of Virginia, where I studied, and I heard his words, "I am the light of the world" (John 8:12). I claimed his promise of "Peace I leave with you, . . . not as the world [gives]" (John 14:27 KJV). And I heard his warning: "Not everyone who says to me 'Lord, Lord' will enter the kingdom" (Matthew 7:21).

My mind then went to the great hymn of Charles Wesley. How can the chains of our racism fall off? How can our hearts, the hearts of all of us, be freed?

Then Bishop Lewis led us in a service of reclaiming our baptismal vows. We were all seated next to each other in a circle, and we asked the questions of one another. And so, Bishop Hope Morgan Ward on one side of me asked me the question:

"Ken, do you renounce the spiritual forces of wickedness, reject the evil powers of this world, and repent of your sin?"

And I answered, "Yes."

And then she asked, "Do you accept the freedom and power God gives you to resist evil, injustice, and oppression in whatever forms they present themselves?"

And I answered, "Yes."

I touched the water and placed it on my forehead, and then asked these same questions of Bishop Bill McAlilly who was seated on the other side of me. And on it went, around the circle.

As bishops we have been consecrated to give spiritual leadership to The United Methodist Church in the Southeast. Bishop James Swanson of Mississippi challenged us, the white members of the college and especially the white males, to speak. And so, I will add to what I had said earlier in social media: We remember the heritage of slavery, racism, injustice, and genocide, but we do not celebrate it. We can only celebrate the gospel of Jesus Christ who is the Lamb of God who takes away the sin of the world (John 1). We can confess that we have sinned, in what we have done and what we have left undone. We can confess that our complicity in this history has compromised our witness to the God who has created us all in God's image (Genesis 1). And in these dark days of our beloved nation, we can claim the promises of our baptism, which is our primary identity—in Christ—and ask our Lord for the power to become the people we profess to be.

Moving forward, and from a strategic perspective, we will benefit if evangelical and progressive Christians find common ground and voice in saying "no" to the alt-right movement and white supremacy. This is happening, if we are willing to listen. And the seriousness of this form of prejudice, bigotry, and heresy requires that we get out of our ideological camps and echo chambers and stand in the gap for those who are the targets of this kind of racism. And that we appreciate those who are willing to stand in the gap with us, but who might not begin at the same place or know our motivations or experience or theories. And this is happening too.

We need deeper understanding. We need to know the history of our nation, especially the history of the American South. We need to know the history of national socialism. We need to know the heresy of racism and misappropriation of Scripture that led to our divisions as Methodists, and we need to read the Barman Declaration, which was a theological response to the Nazi movement. The persistence of strains of white supremacy combined with violence is a threat to the world that God loves. We need statements. We need to speak with moral clarity, and our words are best shaped by the deep well of the biblical prophets (Micah 6:8). I ask preachers to speak clearly from the pulpit, from the Scriptures about where we find ourselves in this present moment. At the same time, we avoid self-righteousness—all have sinned (Romans 3; Isaiah 6). We can speak prophetically and with humility. We use the language of "us" and not "you" when we call for repentance and conversion of the heart and mind. But we cannot be silent. If we are silent the stones will cry out (Luke 19:40).

I also find Richard Rohr's insight to be compelling: "The best criticism of the bad is the practice of the better. Oppositional energy only creates more of the same." So how do we create multicultural churches where people of all races read the Bible together, pray together, worship together, watch over one another in love, and speak the truth in love together? How do we create such churches that by their very existence make the kinds of marches that happened in Charlottesville absurd? These churches exist, all across Florida and the rest of the United States. And before you lament that not enough of them exist, how are you helping to create one of them?

We need to create Christian communities that embody an alternative to hatred, as expressed, for example, in the words of Jesus in the Beatitudes (Matthew 5:1-12). We are called to be the salt of the earth and the light of the world (Matthew 5:13-16). And this will happen as we open our Bibles, as we kneel at our altars, as we receive the grace of the body of Christ, and, yes, as we will fulfill the promises of our baptisms.

I join you in prayer for our church and our nation, even as I remember the words of Thomas More's "For Grace to Labor":

> "The things, good Lord, that we pray for, give us the grace to labor for."
>
> *(The United Methodist Hymnal, 409)*

# 10

# NEGOTIATING FOR MUTUAL BENEFIT

I have benefited from several opportunities for continuing education that came at just the right time in my life. I spent a year in Ed Friedman's seminar on family systems when I was in my late twenties. I learned a great deal from Ken Callahan about leadership and mission in my thirties. Particular laypersons came along when I needed their gifts—Jane Sharp and Jace Ralls of Christ Church in Greensboro; Linda Tatum, Carol and David DeVries of St. Timothy's in Greensboro; and Walter and Michele Fisher and Wanda and Bill Musgrave at Providence in Charlotte are examples.

As I began serving as a bishop, I recognized that I needed another kind of training. I often found myself in conversations with attorneys, activists, and the media in some recurring conflicts—open or closed meetings, clergy retirements, church closures, church-school relationships, how protests occurred in public meetings, staff disagreements.

I had heard of the Harvard Program on Negotiation and made the journey to take part in their three days of training in 2017. This would prove very beneficial to me in the Way Forward, as president of the Council of Bishops, and in the ministry of seeking just resolutions to complaints.

Some of what I learned:

- Negotiations fail when we think there must be winners and losers. The goal is to help each person and party gain as much as they need.

- In any negotiation there are three domains in play—substance, process, and relationships. Substance includes covenants, benefits, resources. Process is how we talk about the substance and whose voice is heard. Relationships is how we manage our differences. We should not confuse substance and relationships.
- It is important to listen for the interests underneath the positions. When we do this, we expand our range of options. In this way we are always searching for models of mutual benefit. This involves clarity about one's direction but having as much flexibility as possible about execution.

My clarity came to be about the essential goal of removing the discriminatory language about homosexuality in *The Book of Discipline*. This could occur through a distributed authority to regional (central) conferences, but more likely a separate denomination and more robust annual conferences.

There are real questions of substance, and some of these can be determined by impartial arbitration. This would happen later under the guidance of Kenneth Feinberg.

On the question of mutual benefit . . .

What would most benefit the traditionalists are:

1. a pathway for local churches to remain in their buildings;
2. a narrative that is about setting them free to multiply their mission;
3. an ongoing relationship to the pension program; and
4. a fair allocation of resources that they have contributed to, but not at the expense of harming others or compromising the next generation of mission.

What would most benefit centrists and progressives are:

1. removal of the restrictive language around LGBTQ persons;
2. a pathway to the new connection;

3. the skills and practices not to devour each other (centrists and progressives) in the process;

4. in the interim, likely two to three years, a moratorium on LGBTQ trials (this would need to be tied to the trust clause for traditionalists); and

5. a real conversation about sustainability for the next generation of mission and the vitality of diverse local churches.

Staying at the table, continuing to seek mutual benefit, would be essential. In theory I learned this in the Harvard Program on Negotiation. I would later experience it in practice in the Protocol on Reconciliation and Grace through Separation.

# 11

# BORN ON THE 4TH OF JULY

Presiding at an annual conference is intense. The meeting of the Florida Annual Conference in the summer of 2017 had gone well. I have always intentionally sought to bring together a diverse slate of presenters, and at this gathering Elaine Heath, Kevin Watson, and Bishop Pereira from Cuba had spoken. The session concluded with the service of commissioning and ordination on Saturday morning. Afterward, I was exhausted.

A few days later I would fly to Santa Clara, Cuba, to speak to the annual conference of the Methodist Church of Cuba, in the company of Icel and Armando Rodriguez, two amazing servants of God. And by Monday of the next week I was sitting on the porch of our mountain cabin at Lake Junaluska, North Carolina. The cabinet had arrived and we were led in a retreat on resilience by my friend, Bishop Janice Huie.

The Junaluska retreat, following our annual conference by a week each year, had become a tradition of relaxation and learning for all of us. Our leaders looked forward to escaping the Florida heat in June, and it was a way of getting on the balcony, in the language of Ronald Heifetz, and thinking long term about our life and work together.

After the retreat concluded I drove to Charlotte and met a writing team composed of just a few members of the Commission on the Way Forward. We worked for two days, and I then drove to Durham, North Carolina, to see the Durham Bulls baseball team with our daughter Abby, who was expecting a child within a few days! I then headed back to Lake Junaluska.

2016    2017    2018    2019    2020

My life has truly been blessed with friendships. I spent one long afternoon with Jamie Armstrong and Elizabeth Graves, lifelong clergy friends. Jamie had been very ill. Soon Elizabeth would be diagnosed with cancer, and she would die within two years. I had lunch with Bishop Lawrence McCleskey at one of our favorite restaurants. That evening I saw the Asheville Tourists, another baseball team, with my friend Mike Rich. The next evening I had dinner with Linda Tatum, Carol and David DeVries, and Jane Sharp, four close friends from Greensboro, who were at the assembly for a retreat.

It was a wonderful week apart, spending time with friends and seeing Balsam Range, one of my favorite bluegrass groups, in concert. One morning I sketched out this prayer:

> O God,
> give me the strength to run this race
> give me the awareness of mentors and encouragers
> give me the patience to stay in these conversations
> give me the grace to appreciate others
> give me the capacity to let go of whatever is not of you
> give me the courage to carry your cross
> and give me the hope of a risen and glorified life in your
> presence.
> In the name of Jesus, the pioneer and perfecter of our faith.
> Amen.

At Junaluska I do sense that I am surrounded by a cloud of witnesses (Hebrews 12:1). I think of James Bellamy, with whom our family stayed when we were young and had little money. I think of Jim Faggart, who along with James stood with me when I was ordained and who died this past year (I had missed that). And I think of Professor Tom Langford, whose thinking and way of understanding our tradition continue to be helpful to me.

My friend George Mitrovich was to preach at Long's Chapel, at Lake Junaluska, on Sunday of that week. He had a health event and called to ask if I could preach in his place. I told him that the invitation needed to come from Chris, the pastor, but that I would be honored to do this. And I mentioned that our first grandchild was scheduled to be born very soon following that service. It might be that I would preach and depart very quickly!

The pastor at Long's Chapel did invite me to preach, and after preaching three times on that Sunday morning, I ate a quick lunch and headed east. My family all gathered in Durham. My daughter Abby would go into the hospital the next day, on Monday.

We slept in, took our time, and went to lunch at an outdoor restaurant near Duke University. It was a beautiful setting. I ordered a Carolina burger (with slaw and chili), sweet potato fries, and unsweet tea.

We then drove to Duke North Hospital. Paige would not come that evening. We went home and slept. We were all in the waiting room again on Tuesday, waiting for Paige.

She would arrive that day, which happened to be July 4th. Paige Elizabeth Stanton, 8.5 pounds, 20.5 inches, and healthy, along with her mother. I praised God!

That evening we drove from the hospital to Abby and Allen's house, to rest for the night. And as we passed through the city it was obvious that Paige's birth had captured the imagination of the entire city. People had lined the streets to celebrate, and they would later shoot off fireworks!

I shared their joy. There is nothing like being a grandparent!

# 12

# TWO CONGREGATIONS

I n September 2017, Hurricane Irma struck Florida. The Florida Conference had strong teams and clear processes in place as we anticipated the
coming of the storm. A call center would be functional and superintendents had plans of action for their districts.

I urged pastors to communicate more, not less, about how the local
church would be present and in mission during these days. Some would open
their homes to colleagues and friends. Some were in the process of evacua-
tion. I asked us to err on the side of patience and generosity with each other.

In Romans 12, Paul writes:

> Do not lag in zeal, be ardent in spirit, serve the Lord.
> Rejoice in hope, be patient in suffering, persevere in prayer.
> Contribute to the needs of the saints; extend hospitality to
> strangers (vv. 11-13).

The call was to be safe, stay connected, and remain prayerful. God
would be with us.

And then the storms came.

Many of our folks were without power. There was significant wind and
flood damage in some areas of the conference. And in the days ahead we
would attend to these congregations and communities.

Some passed through the storm and were grateful. Others like us
anticipated a long night in an interior space, but with lower level (but still

serious) winds. Our peak time—we are thirty minutes east of Tampa—was from about midnight to five a.m.

So, we lit a candle and said a prayer of thanksgiving. God would be with us.

## WEATHERING THE STORM

As dawn emerged, it turned out that Irma had come directly through Lakeland the night before. While it was intense, at the same time there was no significant damage in our home. We were grateful and took a deep breath. The sun was shining.

We got in touch with staff and retired clergy, and district superintendents began contacting their pastors. Some wind damage and flooding was evident. Most had a loss of power and some areas remained restricted. There would be a great deal of chaos as several million people transitioned back to their homes.

We began a conversation with UMCOR about an emergency grant, and our staff were at work getting the call center in operation (this had to do with power). Some areas of our state were still experiencing Irma, especially the Northeast District (Jacksonville), where the flood potential was very real. We learned more about the Miami and Fort Lauderdale areas as the day went on. A few communities were of great concern to us and we were still trying to connect with them.

We would soon have coordinated sites across the conference from which to do ministry. We wanted a seamless transition into being the hands and feet of Jesus in our communities. We were grateful for the connection and prayers from around the church; they were a great source of strength. Pam and I have been so blessed by friends across a lifetime who have been in churches with us, and now by the amazing people of the Florida Conference.

## VISITING IN THE AFTERMATH

After the storm, we ventured out. First, we made a 325-mile round trip from Lakeland to Naples to Immokalee to Sebring and back to Lakeland, basically following the path of the entry of Hurricane Irma onto the peninsula of Florida, along the Highway 27 corridor.

We met with pastors and lay leaders. We prayed in English and Spanish. We talked with community leaders and a mayor who happens to work with youth in her United Methodist Church. We saw homes surrounded by water and sanctuaries drenched by the flood. We stood with people who had no clean water, no electricity, no internet access, no air conditioning. Some had no immediate prospects for any of this. We heard testimonies of broken people who are already feeding hundreds in their communities. At times it was honest and raw. At times it was healing and almost hopeful.

We offered the services of Disaster Recovery, Ministry Protection, and UMCOR, but mostly we listened to the personal sacrifices and struggles and out of that the refusal to despair among these leaders of congregations and communities. We formed circles of prayer and every single person spoke to God, out of the storm and its aftermath.

The next day we headed in the opposite direction, toward Jacksonville, also flooded. And in a couple of weeks I visited Miami and the Keys.

We heard many stories of communities in Florida that seemed to come through the storm intact. We spent time with people whose lives, homes, and churches were devastated. I was in awe of their courage and faith.

## TWO CONGREGATIONS

As a bishop, I am called to search for the signs of vitality and new life in the churches. Often this is the transition from attractional to missional church.

The Florida Conference was devastated by Hurricane Irma, which displaced 2.8 million people across our state. As soon as we were able, we drove around the peninsula and met with people, usually inside buildings with no power or outside, mostly in groups of five or ten or fifteen people.

One day we were inside a church. There was no electricity. The watermarks revealed the damage of the flood. We were all exhausted and overwhelmed—overwhelmed people caring for overwhelmed people.

We were there to listen. A leader began to speak.

> We have no power. We can't meet in the church. We don't expect to have power for a long time. All of the food in our freezers has gone bad, so we can't have church meals. We look forward to getting everything turned on again so we can get back to church.

We listened. We joined hands. We prayed. We embraced. We said goodbye.

About an hour away we came to another church. There were about ten of us. Again, we were there to listen. A woman began to speak.

> We have lost our home. It can't be replaced, but we are alive. That is what matters. We have no electricity, no power, and we knew our food would go bad. So we all took our grills out onto the street, and fired them up and took out all of the food we had, and every night was like a party, a feast. We had Cuban food, barbecue, Brazilian food, and we met neighbors we had never gotten to know.

And then, she said, *"It was like the kingdom of God."*

We are called to be the church of Jesus, who fed the multitudes, to give all we have, as a sign of God's kingdom. We have the Scriptures, we have a table with bread and wine, we have the gospel, we have real people with gifts and talents.

Vital congregations make disciples who transform the world. The hurricane and later the pandemic would reveal that we are all spiritually hungry, inside and outside our churches. Something new is taking shape.

A blended ecology of what we have inherited and what we are called to innovate. Digital technologies would remind us that the church is not closed but being used in a new way. God is never without a witness.

## A DILEMMA

Some bishops love to fly on airplanes. I am not one of them. It could be a factor of being six feet six inches tall. And it could be my sense of being rooted in a place.

One afternoon not long after Hurricane Irma, I departed for six days in Berlin. It would be the fifth of nine meetings of the Commission on a Way Forward. Meeting in Berlin allowed our African members to have a trip that was only half their usual distance.

When Irma was coming, I could have imagined not making this meeting. But as our response unfolded I realized that it was a commitment I needed to keep. Great people were doing the work, the response was moving forward in an almost "viral" way, and it was a marathon, not a sprint.

Most importantly, as I met with pastors and lay leaders in the wake of the storm, I heard them speak of the connection we have as United Methodists. When we need each other, at our best, we are there for each other. My work with the Commission on a Way Forward was in service of that connection. I did and continue to do this work for people who express their faith in Jesus among the most vulnerable in their communities through this imperfect denomination. And over and over again God chooses to use us.

This is what motivates me to find a way forward.

# 13

# AFRICA COLLEGE OF BISHOPS

I had been invited by Bishop John Yambasu, president of the African College of Bishops and resident bishop of Sierra Leone, to speak with the bishops of Africa about the Way Forward. They would be meeting on the campus of Africa University.

I had been to Africa University once before and had always found this to be one of the most compelling ministries of our denomination. Years earlier I had come to know and enjoy friendship with Jim Salley, the extraordinary layperson from South Carolina who had spearheaded the development work on behalf of the school. He and Bishop Lawrence McCleskey had arranged for Providence UMC in Charlotte to host the Africa University Choir as they sang in our worship services. Jim preached there one World Communion Sunday, and we raised funds to construct a faculty residence. Pam and I had gone there to see that work, and later Florida would begin to gather funds for a scholarship in the Institute of Peace, Leadership, and Governance.

As I sat with the bishops at the beginning of their meeting, I knew this would be significant for the work of finding a way forward. They introduced me, and of course I knew them, several much better than others. Three members of their college were on the Commission on a Way Forward—Bishops Niwathiwa, Muyombo, and Yohanna. Bishop David Yemba was also present.

I began by thanking them for the invitation. From the university, it is a very long journey to Old Mutare, Zimbabwe. The flight from Atlanta to

Johannesburg, I am told, is the longest flight in the Delta Airlines system. Yet, I was grateful to be in that space.

After thanking them, I said a word about the US church, in its complexity and yet also in its struggle with the present *Book of Discipline*, and my role as a moderator of the commission. I was not there to persuade them in their thinking about homosexuality, I told them. I was primarily there to listen.

And so, I then said that I wanted to hear from each of them. I asked them to talk from their own context about the way forward and what was important to their areas. Africa is a massive continent with a profound diversity across cultures. I also asked them to talk about matters essential to the mission in their areas, which they are often not able to discuss in a Council of Bishops meeting.

And then I said, "I am not going to speak, until every one of you has spoken. I want and need to hear from each of you."

We began in the early morning. And our conversation flowed for the next day and a half. They spoke of Ebola and Boko Haram, of mudslides and famine. They spoke of divisions and tribalism. They spoke of colonialism and poverty. And the conversation moved to a deeper place. They spoke of the importation of US initiatives into their areas by US groups, the infusion of money into the leadership of some parties in their conferences who wanted to divide the church, and the way they felt stereotyped and judged by others in the council.

I listened and learned. They were my teachers.

That evening we shared at an outdoor barbecue. I sat and talked with several of the bishops. And more than one bishop said, to me, "It would be very African to say nothing about homosexuality in our *Book of Discipline*."

Two years later, I would ask if I could again meet with the African College, this time at a Council of Bishops meeting at Lake Junaluska, in the fall of 2019. We sat down to lunch, and again Bishop Yambasu led us in a prayer of thanksgiving for the food.

At that meeting in 2019 I offered an opening statement. I apologized for a church that had blamed and judged them after the 2019 General

Conference. I acknowledged that in the Council we had not often focused on missional matters that greatly affected their lives and people. But I also stated, very clearly, that I was not in favor of the dissolution of The United Methodist Church. The language that had become very important to me was "missional partnerships," and I listed some of them—Virginia and Mozambique, Greater New Jersey and Tanzania, Baltimore-Washington and Zimbabwe, Florida and East Angola, West Ohio and the Congo, and I went on. I said, "The stream of the church that wants to maintain the unity of the church, and not the dissolution of the church includes the bishops and leaders who have been in missional partnership with you. It is a mission of giving and receiving. And I want to say to you, this is not about how you vote, that if you vote with us we will be in partnership with you. We have been in mission with you in the past. We are in mission with you now. And we want to be in mission with you in the future. One of the most important aspects of being United Methodists for many of us is our missional partnership with you."

Then, I asked if they would each speak. And they did, honestly, about both their pain and their hopes for the future of the church. We are on the way to becoming a global church, but we are not there yet. The journey involves understanding and misunderstanding, speaking our own truth but listening to the context of our neighbor, and patient and sustained conversation. Some of this conversation would bear fruit later, in initiatives that came to be led from outside the US and gave us a pathway to help move beyond the Way Forward.

# 14

# SPEAKING TO THE JUDICIAL COUNCIL: THE ONE CHURCH PLAN

The Council of Bishops had asked the Judicial Council to make a declaratory decision on the three plans that would come before the upcoming Special Session of the General Conference—the One Church Plan, the Connectional Conference Plan, and the Traditional Plan. Cynthia Fierro Harvey and I flew to Zurich, Switzerland, where the meeting would take place. Europe is a setting that honors the travel especially of African members of the Council, and most of the members live and serve outside of the United States. Tom Lambrecht, Tom Berlin, and Pat Miller, all members of the Commission on the Way Forward, were present. We were also greatly assisted by Bill Waddell, the legal counsel of the Council of Bishops.

I had never spoken before Judicial Council and would never have anticipated the experience.

I gave a theological framework for the One Church Plan, which had been supported by the Council of Bishops. I reflected on *The Book of Discipline*, 2016; ¶¶ 102 (Our Doctrinal Heritage), 105 (Our Theological Task), and 125 (Mission and Ministry of the Church). I noted that our doctrinal standards do not speak of gender identity, human sexuality, or marriage, leaving that as a task of interpretation.

Faced with diverse interpretations of the apostolic message, leaders of the early church sought to specify the core of Christian belief in the canon of Scripture and the creeds (*Discipline*, 102). Nourished by these common roots, of a shared Christian heritage, the branches of Christ's church have developed diverse traditions that enlarge our store of shared understandings (102).

I see diversity as a strength, admitting that some view it as a problem—our lack of uniformity. We are a denomination of twelve million persons on four continents, and yet within nations there are sharp divisions, and some of these divisions have nothing to do with religion. Our calling at the moment was to remain one body in Christ with a diversity of gifts. I noted that Methodism did not arise in response to a doctrinal dispute, although there were and are theological controversies. Wesley's normative response is found in the concept of the catholic spirit, where he speaks of orthodoxy as a slender part of religion, at best. Our calling has not been to reformulate doctrine, but to call people to experience the justifying and sanctifying grace of God. This was and is our missional evangelism, doctrine in service of discipleship.

While the church considers its doctrinal affirmations a central feature of its identity, the church encourages serious reflection across the theological spectrum (*Discipline*, 105). At our best, we are walking in the light of God and walking together. United Methodists are bound by a connectional covenant, integrally holding connectional unity and human freedom (*Discipline*, 125), proclaiming and embodying the gospel in our cultural and social contexts.

Doctrine, I argued, arises out of the life of the church, its faith, its worship, its discipline, its conflicts, its challenges from the world it would serve (105). The One Church Plan removes the recent and modern language about homosexuality that is forty-six years old. It honors and protects traditional conscience. And it helps us to remain in connection for the sake of the mission with those who are not yet a part of any church, who have not yet become a part of the promise of Philippians 2, when every knee will bow and every tongue confess that Jesus Christ is Lord, to the glory of God the Father.

These three disciplinary paragraphs (102, 105, 125) were for me crucial to the way forward: our doctrinal heritage and its relation to our theological task, and how each serves the mission of the church.

After listening to a critique of the One Church Plan, I was offered the opportunity for rebuttal. My primary interest was in protecting the integrity of the plan, which the majority of the Council of Bishops and the Commission on a Way Forward had affirmed. It best captured the purpose of the mission, vision, and scope of the commission, to "maximize the presence of the United Methodist witness in as many places in the world as possible, allowing for as much contextual differentiation as possible, and with a desire for as much unity as possible."

The plan, I noted, did not violate the constitution. It was contextual and constructive. It was future focused and kept us in connection for the sake of the mission. It fulfilled the mandate given to us by the 2016 General Conference.

In the end, the Judicial Council found most of the One Church Plan to be constitutional. I breathed a sigh of relief. The work would be in the hands of the delegates. The council found many core elements of the Traditional Plan to be unconstitutional; some of these were related to due process, and others to enhanced examination and discrimination on one aspect of conduct. One member of the council would later say to me that this was the Council's "Brown vs. Board of Education," in reference to a historic Supreme Court case in the United States.

Of course, all of the work would be amended, brought before the Judicial Council again, and then placed in the hands of the General Conference delegates again, and examined yet again by the Judicial Council. As I prepared to speak to the Judicial Council, I gained a new appreciation for our core doctrinal convictions, for the theological task that brings these into dialogue with our human experience, and with the way this becomes a lived theology for the sake of the mission. This, for me, was precisely where we found ourselves as a denomination, then and now.

# QUESTIONS FOR
# ACCOUNTABLE LEADERS

*I engage in an annual practice of consultations with the members of the Florida Cabinet. We also have two retreats each year—in December and June—and as well as frequent meetings more oriented to our primary tasks (appointment-making, clergy and church systems, administration, connectional ministries).*

On one occasion during my time as moderator of the Commission on a Way Forward, I used these twelve questions as a framework for consultation with the Florida Cabinet, which was shared ahead of the meeting. I have circulated these questions with a number of friends, and each year there are revisions. I have found them helpful in my life, leadership, and context, while working with teams, or as I simply think about accountability and moving forward together with others.

1.  In your leadership area, what initiative/work in progress has the greatest potential to help in fulfilling the mission? Why? (MISSION/PURPOSE)
2.  Who are three to five key leaders with whom you work, and how are you developing stronger relationships and a clearer sense of purpose with them? (SHARED LEADERSHIP)
3.  What are you learning about the culture of the Florida Conference that is a strength? And what are you learning about the culture of the Florida Conference that is

an obstacle to effectiveness, excellence, or fruitfulness? (CULTURE)

4. What one or two changes could help the Florida Conference increase the number of vital congregations and fresh expressions of church? (FOCUS)

5. What training/equipping resources do you need to help in maximizing your own strengths and responding to areas for growth? (SELF-AWARENESS)

6. What do you need to stop doing? Why? (SUSTAINABILITY)

7. Name an incident in your own leadership that speaks to the relationship between empathy and purpose. How did you lead? How might you lead differently? (PERSPECTIVE)

8. How are you using both data and narrative in your discernments and observations? How do we need to change/improve our metrics? (DIAGNOSIS)

9. What would you like to be doing with your life in five years? In ten years? (FUTURE)

10. What would you like to talk about that is not directly related to any of these questions? (OPEN AND CONFIDENTIAL SHARING)

11. (Extra Credit) How are you building trust as a leader? What difficult conversations are you convening? What (small) experiments are you undertaking with the relational capital you are developing? (INNOVATION)

1. How is it with your soul? (SPIRITUAL HEALTH)

# 15

# ANCHORED AND FREE:
# A CHRISTMAS MEDITATION

In his spiritual autobiography, *A Song of Ascents*, written in 1968 at the age of eighty-three, E. Stanley Jones reflects on an insight that came to him earlier in life:

> I was free; free to explore, to appropriate any good, any truth found anywhere, for I belonged to the Truth—to Jesus Christ. My one point of the compass was on Jesus, and the other point could swing as far into truth as it was able. For I was anchored and free!

As 2017 came to a close, I reflected how at Christmas we are anchored in the traditions of familiar Scripture passages, carols, and rituals. And yet there is a freedom as well.

What if the core of the Christmas gospel is that the Word became flesh: one point of the compass is the Word that was God, that was in the beginning (John 1:1), and the other point of the compass is the Word that became flesh and lived among us (John 1:14)?

What if God is both anchored and free, unchanging and always adaptive to human need?

What if God is most glorified on a night like Christmas Eve, when the gathered congregation includes those who are most anchored in the church's life and those who are most often far away, and yet who find themselves drawn to carols, candlelight, and Communion?

What if these two points of the compass bring out the best in all of us—those who are anchored are most open to the stranger, the refugee, and the returning prodigal, while those who are farthest away (in the apostle Paul's language in Ephesians 2, the gentiles) are seeking truth and hungering for a tradition?

What if these two points of the compass demonstrate the sacred journey—we process to the altar, we kneel, we lay our gifts before the Holy Family—and, at the same time, God is moving toward us— "The word became flesh and blood, / and moved into the neighborhood" (John 1:14, *The Message*)?

To be anchored and free is to be deeply at home in God and in the world, to pray within the walls of the church and to serve beyond them. To be anchored and free is to know the music well enough to improvise. To be anchored and free is to overcome the fears that keep us in our comfort zones. And yet, to be anchored and free is to know the place of shelter, the shadow of his wings, our refuge and strength.

And so we are anchored in basic practices of hearing familiar phrases like "Glory to God in the highest, and peace on earth," and "The light shines in the darkness, and the darkness has not overcome it," singing carols, taking bread into our hands, kneeling at an altar, and receiving light from our neighbor's candle. And in the same moment we are free—free to discover the truth and reality of God wherever we find God, for God is always present, if we have eyes to see and ears to hear.

*Book Two*

# WALKING *to the* END *of* OUR LIGHT

## 2018-2019

# Moderator's Reflection on the Way Forward

*In January 2018, the three moderators of the Commission on a Way, David Yemba, Sandra Steiner Ball, and I, urged United Methodists to reflect on where they see mission at the heart of The United Methodist Church, and how mission would be the most promising framework for resolving conflict. We released the statement below.*

## Mission and the Way Forward in the Season after the Epiphany

At the conclusion of the recent meeting of the Commission on a Way Forward, the members were asked to share three words that expressed their prayer for the church in the present moment. The thirty-two persons reflect the global nature of the church and a profound diversity of gender, age, theological perspectives. They are laity, deacons, elders, and bishops. The three words each shared then helped create a *word cloud*. The more often a word is named, the larger it becomes in the word cloud. (See the results at the top of the following page.)

In the *Mission, Vision and Scope* given to the Commission by the Council of Bishops, we are seeking to "design a way for being church that maximizes the presence of a United Methodist witness in as many places in the world as possible." This vision is deeply rooted in the movement of the gospel from a small village in Bethlehem to the ends of the earth. The revelation of the Christ to the magi (the Gentiles) in Matthew 2 signals the church's calling to share the good news with all people. At our best, this

has been the vocation of a missionary church and is the root of a global church, where we are sent "from everywhere to everywhere" in the name of Jesus.

For reflection:

- What does it mean that the commission sees "mission" at the heart of the way forward for our denomination?
- Could it be that we discover our unity as we are in mission together?
- What if mission became the primary framework for our work in resolving conflict?
- How are we called to be in mission together more fully with our brothers and sisters in the LGBTQ community?
- And what three words would express *your* prayer for the church in the present moment?

*Bishops David Yemba, Sandra Steiner Ball, and Ken Carter*
*Moderator Team of the Commission on a Way Forward*

# 1

# THREE CLERGYWOMEN

Much of my work in 2017 took me beyond the Florida Conference. Once that became apparent, my response was to remove myself from almost every role beyond the annual conference responsibility and the Commission on a Way Forward. And so, in one week I resigned from a foundation board, a denominational committee, and a college presidential search committee. I would ask three colleges to allow designees to serve in my ex-officio role on their boards of trustees. Jenn Stiles Williams served wonderfully in this way at Wesleyan College in Macon, Georgia, and Alex Shanks would sit with the trustees of Florida Southern College. Each was a graduate of these institutions.

I was very intentional about being present to Florida, and along the way I saw the gifts of extraordinary clergy. During this season three clergywomen offered remarkable leadership, and their stories inspired others beyond the Florida Conference. As 2018 began and the work of the Commission on a Way Forward continued, the example of these leaders gave me hope for the future.

We had assigned Patti Auperlee to First UMC in Pahokee, Florida. Pahokee is known for resilient people, desperate poverty, and the large number of NFL players the town has produced. Patti arrived in Pahokee and soon discovered a facility, just outside of town, where men who had been designated as sex offenders were housed. Over time, she developed a pastoral relationship with them, came to appreciate their gifts, and in consultation with her leadership and the annual conference protocols on safe sanctuaries, invited them to and integrated them into her church. It was a sign of extraordinary leadership.

The story got out, and a playwright composed a play based on it that was produced off Broadway, entitled "America Is Hard to See." A group of us traveled to New York City to view its opening, and I was honored to be part of a panel discussion. Really I was there to affirm Patti and the people of Pahokee. That evening I would meet Amy Gaither, the daughter of iconic gospel singers and composers, who played Patti's character. I learned that she had come to New York City in part to escape the dark side of celebrity evangelical Christianity, and, in God's providence had auditioned and been selected for a role where she played a clergywoman who exuded the unconditional love of the gospel every night. The play would be performed the next summer at the Fringe Festival in Edinburgh, Scotland, the largest festival in the world.

I also came to know a remarkable leader named Mary Downey, chief executive of the Hope Center in Kissimmee, Florida, adjacent to Orlando. Mary is a deacon and embodies what it means to connect the church and the world. The mission of the Hope Center is to provide affordable housing and to see the dignity in families, especially the working poor

Mary's work became known to a film producer, who embedded a crew in the Hope Center to learn about the mission. This end result was a feature film, *The Florida Project*, which was also the name of the operation that had become Disney World. The film sees daily reality through the eyes of children who live in a precariously dangerous setting within sight of the happiest place in the world for a child. One of the stars of the film was Willem Dafoe.

The Florida Conference sponsored a viewing of the film, and again a panel discussion was held in which I was honored to participate. Like *America Is Hard to See*, *The Florida Project* was both a witness to God's mission, which is compelling in ways that transcend the walls of our churches, and a sign of risk-taking and innovative leadership. Mary would later be named as the Central Floridian of the Year.

I met Audrey Warren early on in Florida. She served as minister of

Branches UMC, an innovative ministry that grew out of an outreach to children in Florida City, below Miami. Her church had burned in a fire, on Pentecost Sunday, and she had led them through a rebuild. The congregation was profoundly multicultural and predominately younger, with a large number of children. I preached on the celebration of their new building, and the next day went on a fourteen-mile bike ride through the Everglades with several people from her church.

During this season I was blogging about the Fresh Expressions movement, even as this was beginning to emerge in Florida. Over the course of a year, I had posted twelve to thirteen pieces and began to see that this could become a book, which Abingdon had agreed to publish. Audrey wrote me amidst this work and told me that she had written Bible studies for each of the posts and had led them in her community.

I quickly realized the book would be much better if we integrated her work and mine. I was helping lead a movement, but she was the practitioner. Abingdon agreed, and so we both revised each other's work, and it became *Fresh Expressions: A New Kind of Methodist Church*.

On days when the denominational process seemed to be at an impasse, I would often reflect on the work that clergy were doing in their own contexts. Patti, Mary, and Audrey were three examples of initiative, creativity, courage, and faithfulness. I would have the awesome privilege of ordaining each of them. And there are many more. A first calling for a bishop is simply to pay attention to what God is doing, and then to support clergy who are leading the church into the profound mission of Jesus Christ.

There is a future with hope.

2016    2017    **2018**    2019    2020

# 2

# THE IMPORTANCE OF CONVERSATION

I came to know Matt Berryman based on a talk I gave to the LGBTQ community and their allies at St. Luke's UMC in Orlando at the end of my first year in Florida (2013). At the time Matt was executive director of Reconciling Ministries Network, an advocacy group for LGBTQ inclusion in The United Methodist Church.

That evening with St. Luke's was at my own initiative; I wanted to begin a conversation. I was graciously received by Bill Barnes and Jenn Stiles Williams, their pastors. A few months afterward, I asked Matt if I could stand with him on the stage at our next annual conference, my second in Florida, introduce him, have him share some of his story, and then offer a prayer for his ministry. He was open to this, for which I was grateful, and we did it in June 2014. I told him before either of us spoke that what people would remember most was that we were simply together.

In 2018, I would sit with Alice Williams and Jorge Acevedo and host a similar conversation at the Florida Annual Conference. Alice, Matt, and Jorge were all members of the Commission on a Way Forward. I know that they shared many deep conversations together.

Below are my words introducing Matt in June 2014, and then the prayer I offered following his witness. Many stood as Matt spoke. Immediately afterward a few thanked me, and a few others objected.

I stand to welcome and introduce Matt Berryman, executive director of the Reconciling Ministries Network. Matt is a Floridian and served churches in Jacksonville and Orange Park. As executive director of the Reconciling Ministries Network, he builds bridges between the LGBT community and local congregations and works for the full inclusion of gay and lesbian Christians in the life of our church.

While Matt and I have different roles and callings in our church, we are united in the conviction that all persons are individuals of sacred worth, created in the image of God, and in our commitment to be in ministry for and with all persons. This conviction motivates me as a bishop and shepherd of the church to be in dialogue and in friendship with Matt.

I had asked Matt to bring a word of greeting, and after he spoke I offered this prayer for his ministry.

Triune God,
nothing can separate us from your love,
which we have come to know
in Jesus Christ our Lord.

We pray now for our brother Matt.

May his ministry of reconciliation
as an expression of your desire for justice and mercy
be a gift to the LGBT community.

May his ministry of reconciliation
in your providence and purpose,
help to build up the One Body.
May the ministry of reconciliation become our passion,
and may our relationships with our brothers and sisters

in the LGBT community
be grounded in your compassion.

Amen.

In the summer of 2018, I had a conversation with Billy Abraham of Southern Methodist University. I was attending my third Oxford Institute for Methodist Theological Studies, in Oxford, England. I participated in a working group on evangelism and gave a plenary address on the Way Forward. The Oxford Institute, held every five years, draws scholars and leaders from throughout the world.

One evening we had just concluded worship in the Christ Church Cathedral, where John and Charles Wesley had worshipped as students and were ordained. We sang, prayed, heard a sermon and received the Eucharist. We then remained seated for the beautiful organ postlude.

After the service we began to walk out and I found myself with Dr. Abraham. I had taken his course on Basic Christianity three decades ago. I had used his book, *The Logic of Evangelism*, over a ten-year period when I taught in the Course of Study at Duke. I have a great admiration for him, and he is brilliant, even as we are not in full agreement on all things.

And so, I said to him, "Billy, I have learned a great deal from you. I continue to learn a great deal from you. We may not end up in the same church, but I want you to know that. I'm grateful for your mind and heart, and our friendship."

And he turned to me, smiled, and said, "Ken, keep following your lights. Keep following your lights." And then he said, "The church is going to be fine." He laughed. I smiled. And we walked into the Oxford night.

I met George Mitrovich in Seattle. I had been invited to give a lecture at Seattle Pacific, a wonderful school. We met, and discovered that we shared two passions, the Methodist faith and baseball, often in that order. Over time he would invite me to the Fenway Park Writer's Series, which he founded and where he introduced me to the MLB Network's Brian Kenny (who happens to be a United Methodist). We walked out and touched the Green Monster together.

George invited me to preach (through his pastor) at his church, First UMC in San Diego, a beautiful and historic structure. I arranged this around a meeting of the Commission on a Way Forward and a visit with our daughter, who was at the time a doctoral student in Chinese Linguistics at UCLA. I was warmly received by their pastor and laity, and after lunch I met with a contingent from the Cal-Pac Conference for a lively dialogue.

Later George would organize a Methodist Day in Spring Training with the Red Sox in Fort Myers with ESPN's Tim Kurkjian as the speaker, where I threw out the first pitch. I love Tim Kurkjian's baseball commentary and I thanked him profusely for coming. He looked at me with a knowing smile and said, "Can you really say no to George?" And we both laughed out loud.

George was a layperson who loved to preach, and he did: First Houston, National Cathedral, Church of the Resurrection in Kansas City, Pasadena Community in St. Pete, First Montgomery. He had a career in politics, having been a press aide to Robert Kennedy. He was instrumental in Major League Baseball's recognition of the birthday of Jackie Robinson. He loved his church and our denomination and had ideas about how both could flourish, and further suggestions about my leadership in some of that, which he was willing to share with me. He often pushed the U.S. bishops to speak more clearly about the common good of the people across our nation. His voice would later be crucial for me in the 2020 National Elections.

George wrote a several-hundred-word entry each day entitled "Baseball Notes." He had ideas about the next Democratic nominee for the presidency and talked often with more than one of them. He shared some of my sermons and prayers with many of his friends, and I was honored. He was an encourager.

Our own conversations were always about important and urgent matters, and I count it one of the unexpected gifts along the way that we met and became friends and shared meals in places like Boston and San Diego and Seattle and Tampa. He loved his family and had a wide network of friends, and none of us found ourselves able to say no to him. Not that we would have wanted to. He was eighty-four at his death, and yet physically active, deeply faithful, and intellectually curious until the end. He was a role model in how to stay connected to people, how to stay engaged in politics in a civil manner, and how to live out one's faith. And he loved baseball, especially the Red Sox and the Padres.

I tell George's story because he was important to me (he would die in July, 2019) and because he is an example of remarkable people who love our church, care about our nation, and find time to explore pursuits in life that are joyful. The same can be said of Matt Berryman, Billy Abraham, and the many other servants of God I have been privileged to know and join in conversation through this journey.

# 3

# THE COMMISSION ON A WAY FORWARD CONCLUDES

The Commission on a Way Forward held its last meeting in May 2018, at the General Board of Higher Education and Ministry in Nashville. We needed to adapt to a recent Judicial Council ruling, which, in our interpretation, led us to the sense that the petitions to the General Conference needed to come from our commission and not from the Council of Bishops. And so we revised our work to be in alignment with this unanticipated shift in expectation. It was a bit disorienting, and we were not entirely able to meet this expectation. We were good with that. We had served the church, I believed, to the best of our ability.

We concluded the work with a service of Holy Communion in the Upper Room Chapel. And then Sandra Steiner Ball called us to enter into intimate personal conversations, during which we asked each other for forgiveness for any harm we had done to each other. We granted each other absolution and shared the peace of Christ. I remember conversations with Jessica Lagrone and Matt Berryman, Tom Lambrecht and Brian Atkins, Debbie Wallace Padgett and Donna Pritchard.

We then released each other and would now serve the church that we love in other ways. The report would go through a final revision of details and, after translation, would become public as soon as possible.

There was a powerful sense of detachment in the ritual we had shared. We were letting go of one another. We were honoring one another's different callings going forward. And we were placing the work now in the hands of the authorized delegates to the 2019 General Conference.

I was deeply grateful to Jorge Acevedo and Alice Williams, both Floridians and members of the commission, and to Alex Shanks, who was the project manager.

I then flew from Nashville to Durham, North Carolina. I would meet Pam there, celebrate our daughter Abby's birthday, and take our granddaughter Paige to see the Durham Bulls, her first baseball game!

Then I would fly home to Florida, where I would preach that weekend in the Villages and meet with June Edwards, Michael Beck, and Fresh Expressions leaders in the North Central District. Michael would become one of the instrumental figures in the Fresh Expressions movement. And early in the next week I would lead a retreat in our home in Lakeland with those whom I would have the great honor to ordain a month later at annual conference.

# 4

# INSTALLATION AS PRESIDENT
# OF THE COUNCIL OF BISHOPS

The completion of the work of the Commission on a Way Forward would coincide with my taking up a two-year role as president of the United Methodist Council of Bishops. Pam and I were present for the service, beautifully led by Bishop Tracy Smith Malone.

My friend Bruce Ough would complete his two-year term as president, which had begun in Portland, Oregon, at the General Conference. He and I had talked on an almost weekly basis. I had been elected to the president designate role three years earlier, as we met in Berlin. Now it had become official. I would serve as president for the next two years, a time that would contain two General Conferences. And Cynthia Fierro Harvey would succeed me, the first Latina bishop to serve in this role.

The Council of Bishops includes sixty-seven active bishops and about ninety retired bishops who serve twelve million members on four continents. The role of president is very much one of being first among equals, if that! It is a designation of a bishop who will serve the bishops, preside in the meetings, and upon occasion speak for the council—although I tried to restrain myself here, sensing that bishops lead and interpret in their own contexts. In our polity I noted that I was grounded in a continuing prayer for the unity of the church, the faithfulness of the church, and the fruitfulness of the church. That evening I received the gavel, the affirmation of the bishops, and the responsibility in a very uncertain time.

In our polity, the role of president is exercised alongside the task of serving an episcopal area, in my case Florida. For those who know me or my work, this could not have been done without the extraordinary gifts of Rev. Alex Shanks, my administrative assistant. Alex had begun in this role in 2016. He had previously been a highly effective pastor in Coral Springs, Florida, near in proximity to Parkland High School, which would become noteworthy for a mass shooting years later. Alex served as a project manager for the Commission on a Way Forward and as a "chief of staff" in the Florida Cabinet, which itself serves a large and diverse conference. And he would attend, with permission of the bishops, each council meeting. Alex's leadership and friendship was and remains a gift.

I had not aspired to the role of president of the council, being relatively new to the work, but I welcomed the opportunity to serve and tried to do my best over the next years. In this role one is often in conversation with the Judicial Council, the News Service, general secretaries of boards and agencies, and advocacy groups. I always tried to imagine how anything I might say or do would be heard in the four-point charge—Prospect, New Home, Shady Grove, Mount Pleasant—I had served in Yadkin County, North Carolina. I tried to respond with a handwritten note to each letter I received.

And I did remind myself that it was a role that had a beginning and an ending. I found myself praying for bishops by name more than I had before. And in this season I would go back to core experiences and principles. I was saved by the grace of God, through faith. When I was baptized I died to self. When I came into the church I was aware that it was not my church. The church is Jesus's body, purchased with his blood. When I was called to ministry it was a privilege. When I became a bishop, it was to do this work for others. I am blessed to know Jesus Christ. I am blessed to be a part of The United Methodist Church. I am blessed with the opportunity to do this work. Now, I would be blessed to serve over one hundred bishops, and by extension the larger church. I was blessed to be a blessing. Was it all perfect? No. But was it well with my soul? Yes.

# 5

# The Gospel of the Burnt Ends

June is usually a busy month, but one week in June 2018 was especially full. I was exhausted by Saturday morning. In fact, I could not remember being that tired. We had had a three-day cabinet retreat, which was great. I had spoken to a group of more than one hundred young adults, had a day trip to Atlanta, and was scheduled to speak to the Western North Carolina Conference on Saturday morning. The week before, I had been in Kentucky and California. And the week before that was the Florida Conference.

Bob Tuttle and I had arranged to have lunch on Saturday, after my scheduled speech with the Western NC Conference. I spoke from 9:30 to 10:30, went back to our place, changed into casual clothes, and planned to take him to Haywood Smokehouse, my favorite BBQ restaurant in Waynesville, North Carolina, near Lake Junaluska. There were some things I wanted to talk with him about and some things he wanted to talk with me about. Bob Tuttle has been my spiritual director, and we have read the Bible together over extended times. We met years ago—he is an elder in the Western North Carolina Conference—but he has also had a profound influence on many in the Florida Conference as a professor at Asbury Theological Seminary.

So, I picked Bob up and took him to the restaurant. It was crowded, it always is. We were open to the first available table. It turned out to be outside, in the shade. This was OK. It was a big picnic table that could seat six. We sat down on one end. I was looking forward to a personal conversation, maybe even with some confession, after a long and busy week

Then the waitress came over. "There is a man over there, by himself, and he was actually before you. Could he sit at this table?" We said sure, and we meant it. But inside I was wondering, "Will we be able to talk?"

So, the man came over and turned out to be friendly. He runs a small construction company in Asheville. Bob and I talked about someone we both knew in Florida, but then we got back to including the man.

"Are you married?" Bob asked him. He was he said. His wife was the great blessing his life. "Do you have children?" They are adults, he talked about them. We talked about our wives and children.

Then later Bob asked about his work. He talked about it.

"It's a beautiful day," the man said. It truly was a beautiful mountain day. "You're right," Bob said. "A friend of mine made this day!" We all laughed. The man said, "You are right."

And then our food came. BBQ brisket. The burnt ends. I highly recommend them.

Bob asked him "Do you go to church?" He did not, anymore.

Bob listened. By now the guy knew we were ministers. He had apologized for drinking a beer, and we told him no problem. There are bigger fish in the world to fry.

We talked some more.

Then Bob asked him, "What would it take to get you to go back to a church?"

And he talked about the internal problems that had led him to leave the church, a Baptist church.

But then he said, "I miss it."

"And your wife is the greatest blessing in your life?" Bob said to him. He nodded and smiled. "Absolutely," he said.

Bob then said, "I am going to pray for you for thirty days." By now Bob knew the man's and his wife's names. And had his phone number to text him.

"I am going to pray for you for thirty days. You will find a church because you can do this for your wife."

Then the man said, "I think you and my wife are connected in all of this."

"Your wife and I have the same friend," Bob said, with a big smile on his face, like he was letting us in on a secret.

I said, "I don't think it was an accident that we were seated together today." And the man said, "Absolutely right." He was smiling.

Then he said, "The five years I was in church were the best five years of my life. I read the Bible every day."

We talked some more and finished most of our meal.

Then the bill came. Bob said, to me, "I am going to get your lunch." And I said, "Only if I can get his." And the man said, "This has turned out to be a pretty great day!" To which Bob said, "It will be a great day if you and your wife can worship together in a church. You can do that for her, right?" And he said, "Yes, I can."

And so, when we left we prayed for him. Bob blessed him. He put his hand on the man's head and blessed him. He also actually placed the man's hand on his own head.

I told him that he had done more for us than we had done for him. And I thanked him for eating with us. We shook hands and said goodbye. He walked to his truck. There was a smile on his face.

We went inside to pay the bill. Bob ended up paying for all of it.

The conversation Bob and I were going to have could wait for another day.

One benefit from reading this is that when you are there you should order the burnt ends of the brisket. They will bring them, but you have to ask.

I do have a lingering question:

Who was the stranger who joined us when we sat down to break bread together at the Haywood Smokehouse?

2016     2017     **2018**     2019     2020

# A Call to Discipleship: Living as Disciples of a Nonviolent Lord in a Time of Violence

*In 2018, I shared the following as a letter from the president of the Council of Bishops and with the Florida Conference as a call to discipleship, specifically a call to nonviolence in a time of violence:*

In my role as president of the Council of Bishops, but more fundamentally as one who professes faith in Jesus Christ as Lord and Savior, I write with a call to discipleship.

The United States has witnessed a steady occurrence of mass shootings across our nation, this past weekend in El Paso, Texas, and Dayton, Ohio. I commend the statements of Bishop Gregory Palmer and Bishop Earl Bledsoe to the people of their residential areas (West Ohio, New Mexico/ Northwest Texas). The carnage following these acts of violence reminds us of Sandy Hook and Orlando, Sutherland Springs and Charlotte, Las Vegas and Parkland, Charleston and Pittsburgh, and on it goes.

Underneath the violence is a culture of white supremacy and a fear of immigrants (xenophobia). These are expressions of our sinful nature and deny the image of God (Genesis 1) that is in every person. Christ died for all (2 Corinthians 5), and in this he loved us and gave himself up for us (Ephesians 5).

I also join my voice with Bishop LaTrelle Easterling of the Baltimore-Washington Conference. The president's disparaging comments about an honorable congressman and a major northeastern city (Baltimore) are rooted in a cynical desire to divide us along racial lines. The use of the presidential role granted for the purpose of serving an entire people for white privilege does great harm to us. According to counterterrorism experts, the president's racial rhetoric is fueling an incipient and violent white nationalist movement in our nation.

The majority of our membership in the US is Anglo. If you are a white person reading this and you find it troubling—in my own self-examination and confession, I do, as I am under the same judgment—I urge you not to write me, but to contact a friend who is black or Latino/a and ask them, "What did you hear in these statements?" and "What do you perceive in these mass shootings?"

I write less to reinforce our very real political partisanship and more to say that we can have a better civil dialogue, and perhaps United Methodists who are Democrats and Republicans in the United States can contribute to this. We are in desperate need of leadership that does not pit us against each other. And we are in need of a dialogue that is deeply rooted in our discipleship in the way of our nonviolent Lord and Savior, Jesus Christ.

Jesus is calling us to love our neighbor (Mark 12). To love our neighbor is to work for a church that does not exclude anyone, that welcomes immigrants, that reckons with the systemic realities of racism and that honors the faith of people across the political aisle from wherever we are sitting.

To love our neighbor is the cost of discipleship (Dietrich Bonhoeffer). To love our neighbor may be our most powerful form of evangelism at the present moment. To love our neighbor is to move beyond our fragility toward repentance and reform. And of course, all of this leads to the question asked of Jesus by the lawyer in Luke 10, and his surprising and unsettling response. For Jesus, questions of eternal life had nothing to do with separation from or superiority toward the other. As disciples of Jesus in the Wesleyan tradition, holiness is not separation; holiness is love of God and neighbor (*Plain Account of Christian Perfection*, *The Almost Christian*). And we cannot love God, whom we have never seen, if we do not love our brother or sister whom we have seen (1 John 4).

2016    2017    2018    2019    2020

It turns out that the neighbor we are called to love is the one we have profiled and labeled as our enemy. And it turns out that by teaching us to love our enemy (Matthew 5), Jesus is forming us in a holiness without which we will not see the Lord (Hebrews 12).

What is God's dream for us? How can we become the answer to the words we say in worship, "Thy kingdom come, Thy will be done"? (Matthew 6 KJV). In Wesley's words, we are being called "to reform the nation, particularly the church, and to spread scriptural holiness over the land" (from John Wesley's "Large Minutes").

The Council of Bishops is a global body and The United Methodist Church is a global church. I call upon our brothers and sisters in Europe, the Philippines, and Africa to intercede for us in this struggle (1 Thessalonians 5), that we would be faithful, nonviolent and courageous in our discipleship.

And so, I call us to be the people we profess to be: disciples of Jesus Christ for the transformation of the world (*The Book of Discipline*, 2016; ¶120). We pray for healing among those who are grieving, amendment of life among those who have done violence, and judgment upon our human hearts when our spoken words have contributed to violence (Matthew 12). And we commit ourselves to the transformation of systems and laws that reflect the life that Jesus promises (John 10) and to the peace of Christ that breaks down the dividing walls of hostility (Ephesians 2).

# LETTER TO A
# TRADITIONALIST FRIEND

*I wrote this letter to a friend whom I greatly admire, in October 2018. My friend would characterize himself as a traditionalist and an evangelical.*

Dear _____,

Thank you for the breakfast conversation last week. It was a very significant conversation for me. And I learned a lot from you and those who were with us. There is no question in my mind that you are apostolic leaders.

Thank you also for pushing—appropriately, with conviction, truthfully, in mature Christian speech—at a couple of things. For that very reason I value the conversation all the more.

It prompted me to think more and that is why I am writing. Not to explain, not to clear anything up, not to persuade, but to honor the integrity of our friendship, our relationship, and your leadership.

I do live in the tension of interpreting the three plans, that came from the Way Forward, and also communicating in a different way the plan that the COB affirmed, which was the One Church Plan.

I try very hard to place the three plans on a level playing field—this was my work in recruiting people to complete the Traditional Plan, in being open in the executive committee of the COB to taking a step back in including it, in ensuring that it was in a form in the final report that had integrity alongside the other two plans, and in ensuring that the Judicial Council would evaluate its constitutionality alongside the other two. All of this I did because it seemed fair to traditionalist United Methodists who would be on the floor of the General Conference and who would be voting on it. I felt and feel that those votes should be on the merits of the plans.

This is one part of my work. And in the Upper Room Chapel, as the Commission on a Way Forward completed its journey, I was released from some of this work, especially moderating that group.

But it is not the only part of my calling.

I am an advocate of the One Church Plan because, in my own journey, it is the one plan that can possibly keep our church together. As I concluded in that talk with the WNC Annual Conference, it expresses the words in Ephesians 4:3 in the form of a question: "Have we made every effort to maintain the spirit of unity in the bond of peace?"

I am an advocate for the One Church Plan not because I am trying to spin anything ideologically. Rather, because I want us to remain together in one body. And that is living in the tension of less than some want among both traditionalists and progressives. And I completely get that for some of those it is not enough. I can also honor that.

A bishop on the commission and a member of the commission have made similar comments over the past two years.

So, I live in this tension. I had not thought of it in this way until a traditionalist leader, one identified with a movement to walk apart, told me, this year, that this was my calling—to live in the tension of presiding fairly and teaching a way forward.

What I realize I need to make more clear is that I am not trying to create a pathway for anyone to leave, but a way for as many as possible to remain together as one church. This is about removing the language, providing religious protection of conscience, and not requiring anyone to vote or certify someone else's conscience.

In the spirit of convicted humility, I may be wrong here, and I ask God to teach me that. I know that I will be judged by God. If I err on the side of mercy, that will be what I will say to him. If it is not enough, I lay that before God also.

In this life I do believe in the relationship pyramid of *The Anatomy of Peace*. Relationships are not the avoidance of work, but they are often the work itself. Regardless of the outcome, I will always be grateful for the relationships we have, in Christ.

So, again, I write not to explain, not to clear up, not to persuade. This is simply a part of my witness, even as I have benefited from yours.

I write not with a troubled spirit, but with great appreciation. The God who began a good work in us will be faithful to complete it.

Your friend and coworker in Christ,
+Ken

# 6

# HOLINESS REDEFINED

True religion according to John Wesley is happiness, and happiness is true religion. It is the necessary integration of the love of God and neighbor, or what he described as gratitude and benevolence. There is no separation of these two. And as we come to love God and our neighbor more fully, the image of God, which is love, is restored in us. This image is deeply trinitarian: the Father who sends the Son, the incarnate Son Jesus who bears witness to that Creator and who died on the cross that we might have fellowship with God and neighbor through the Holy Spirit, who dwells within us and among us.

The restoration of the image of God is the journey toward holiness. It is not a status. It is not a separation from the impure. Holiness is the purpose for which we were created, to reflect the nature of God. And we cannot make this journey toward holiness alone. This was Wesley's critique of solitary religion, and his affirmation that there is no holiness but social holiness. This means we become more holy as we read Scripture together, take Communion together, confess our sins together, and respond to human needs through acts of mercy and justice together.

We believe that holiness can only truly happen in our lives, and we are more likely to discover happiness in our lives, as we are accountable for the grace that we have received. This is real gratitude. Nothing is our possession—our money, our position, our church. Everything belongs to God and we are stewards. Accountability in the early Wesleyan movement happened in small groups and conferences, and also as early Methodist people practiced the General Rules.

So, if we would pursue holiness—and here I refer not to perfectionism or judgmentalism, but to the life our Creator intends for us—imagine the life we would intend for our loved ones and friends, even for our children and grandchildren. As I have prayed and reflected, the following practices have been helpful to me:

- How can I live out of a sense of gratitude each day? Can I write down at least three specific things each day for which I am grateful?
- How can I become a more loving and giving person? Can I simplify my life and, in the process, give things that I own or have accumulated to others?
- How can I come to the conviction that holiness is happiness, or joy? How can I come to know that happiness is discovering the path that God has chosen for me and walking in that direction?

And who can help me be holy and happy? Can I write down the names of two to three brothers and sisters in Christ who can hold me accountable—who can speak the truth in love to me—for the gifts and grace that surround me?

Were we able to begin to understand and practice holiness in these ways, we would be more Wesleyan, we would be more encouraging of each other, and we would find ourselves happier and more joyful in God, and on a clearer path to holiness.[1]

---

1  I am indebted throughout this reflection to Rebekah Miles, Andrew Thompson, Bob Tuttle, and Paul Chilcote.

# 7

# THE BASEMENT AND
# THE SANCTUARY

I can still remember the day, a few years ago now. It was an unbearably hot summer day in the Deep South of the US. Our life's possessions were in a van, spilling over into a couple of cars and a friend's truck. We were in the process of moving into the parsonage of the church to which I had been assigned.

At some point late in the day I walked across the street to the church's sanctuary; someone had entrusted me with the keys. It was a beautiful space, quiet and peaceful, serene and orderly. I stopped for a moment. Then I made my way through a door, and turned left and then went down some stairs, into a little room, a basement, underneath. It was crowded and dark, scary and disordered.

Every church, I suppose, has a place of beauty, for public worship. And every church, I suppose, has a place of storage, an out-of-the-way place, usually underneath everything else and harder to find. In fact, most people don't even know that it's there.

I thought about that basement as I read the 130th Psalm. *"Out of the depths I cry to you, O LORD"...* (v. 1). And just as there are depths in buildings, there are deep places in our lives as well. This is not the poetry of the quiet and peaceful, the serene and orderly. The psalm really is a cry from the depths, from all that is crowded and dark, scary and disordered in our own lives.

Psalm 130 is a word that goes all the way down to where we live. Some of us, I imagine, have been there. To be depressed is to be pushed down. To be discouraged is to have a deficit of spirit. To be deflated is to have all of the wind taken out of our sails.

We have all been in the basement and in a sanctuary. As bishops, think of the moment you were elected and escorted before a group of people who had just affirmed your call to this office. Think of the moment you knelt and placed your hand on a Bible and someone you had admired and respected laid hands on you and said something encouraging to you.

Those are holy moments. Stay there for a minute. We have all been in that sanctuary.

Now, think of one of the most troubling days in your life as a bishop. The disruption or some chaos that came to you. The violation of human dignity on the part of a clergy. The need to close a church. Or a betrayal. Or an event of national or international importance or a natural disaster. Or the death of someone close to you.

We have all been in those places of chaos. We have all been in those basements.

What do you do?

## DE PROFUNDIS

In the tradition of the Latin, the name for the psalm's first words is *de profundis*, out of the depths, out of the deep. I can hear a choir singing Rutter's *Requiem* here, the bass voices all the way down there, "Out of the deep, have I called unto thee, O Lord."

Perhaps we thought the spiritual life would be the comfort of a sanctuary, safe and secure from all alarms. And then we found or find ourselves in the strange and unfamiliar territory of a dark, damp basement.

What do you do?

You cry out to God. You get in touch with the deepest places. It gets real, even profound. The synonyms for *profound* are severe, deep,

deep-seating, intense, overwhelming. It can relate to a state of emotion. But it can also relate to insight: penetrating, discerning, wisdom.

In the depths, in the chaos, in the overwhelming, we discover who we are. And, theologically, biblically, we discover who we are *in relation to God.*

Perhaps we are in this place of discovery as a Council of Bishops.

Perhaps we are in this place of discovery as a United Methodist Church.

Who can we trust?

Israel's fundamental identity was found in the experience of the Exodus. In the Exodus they called upon the name of the Lord. And the beginning of their salvation was the response: "I have heard the cries of my people." There is an echo of the Exodus in this psalm of ascent, sung as the people walked up together to the Temple in Jerusalem. They remembered their story. They knew their condition, their situation, which was real, but they could place it in a context.

Out of the deepest, most chaotic and overwhelming places, we cry out to you, O Lord. And it is a cry, as the English word *supplication* captures it, for *mercy.* There is a hint here that the condition of the psalmist can be traced, at least in part, to his own sinfulness.

When we have hit bottom, we learn something about ourselves.

When we have hit bottom, we might as well be honest about it.

When we have hit bottom, we can take some responsibility for the situation.

How do we take responsibility, as a Council of Bishops? We return to our sources. We are grounded, even humbled. We remember the words we have led others to say, acknowledging our own need for them:

> We have not loved you with our whole heart.
> We have failed to be an obedient church.
> We have not done your will,
> we have broken your law,
> we have rebelled against your love,

we have not loved our neighbors,
and we have not heard the cry of the needy.[1]

Out of the deep, we cry out.
I want to stay with two phrases in that confession:

We have not loved you with our whole heart.
We have not loved our neighbors.

This is, of course, an echo of Mark 12, the Great Commandment. And these were the very words John Wesley would use to define *holiness*, being made perfect in love. If we are honest, we are not there. We are still being made perfect in love. But we are not there.

Most of us, in this room, would appear to be successes. We were blessed, affirmed, elected, lifted up, set apart.

These are words of failure. We have failed to be an obedient church.

---

1 "A Service of Word and Table I: Confession and Pardon," *The United Methodist Hymnal* (Nashville, TN: The United Methodist Publishing House, 1989), 8.

# 8

# THE BENEFITS OF FAILURE AND THE POWER OF IMAGINATION

In 2008, J. K. Rowling gave the commencement address at Harvard University. She, is of course, one of the world's most influential literary figures. Speaking to that gathering of students and their families, she spoke about her own journey:

> I think it fair to say that by any conventional measure, a mere seven years after my graduation day, I had failed on an epic scale. An exceptionally short-lived marriage had imploded, and I was jobless, a lone parent, and as poor as it is possible to be in modern Britain, without being homeless. The fears that my parents had had for me, and that I had had for myself, had both come to pass, and by every usual standard, I was the biggest failure I knew.

> Now, I am not going to stand here and tell you that failure is fun. That period of my life was a dark one, and I had no idea that there was going to be what the press has since represented as a kind of fairy tale resolution. I had no idea then how far the tunnel extended, and for a long time, any light at the end of it was a hope rather than a reality.[1]

---

1 J. K. Rowling, "The Fringe Benefits of Failure and The Importance of Imagination," https://news.harvard.edu/gazette/story/2008/06/text-of-j-k-rowling-speech/.

She would go on to talk about very real struggles, within herself and outside. She would talk about how she came to know herself, her limitations, her will, her discipline. She got more in touch with the evil that she saw in the world, which gave her nightmares. And she began to see the good in the world.

The title of her address was "The Fringe Benefits of Failure, and the Importance of Imagination."

She says about the benefits of failure: "Failure meant a stripping away of the inessential. I stopped pretending to myself that I was anything other than what I was, and began to direct all my energy into finishing the only work that mattered to me."[2]

## THE POWER OF IMAGINATION

She goes on, in the address, to speak of the power of "imagination." And I want to suggest that, for us, this imagination is the gift of God that gives us the energy to do that only work that matters.

What is the only work that matters for the Council of Bishops in this season?

What is the only work that matters for twelve million United Methodists around the world?

It begins with coming to know God as God really is. Something remarkable happens when we cry out to God. We learn, at the point of our greatest need, a lot about who God really is. The psalmist helps us in verse 3: "If you, O LORD should mark iniquities, / Lord, who could stand?"

When we have experienced failure or are wandering around in some spiritual basement, God is not standing there, sneering at us and saying, "I told you this would happen!"

God is not the author of a blog, constantly writing us and telling us how terrible we are!

God is not a detached philosophical idea, at a distance from us, saying, "I told you so!"

---

2 Rowling, "The Fringe Benefits of Failure and The Importance of Imagination."

When we have hit bottom, we discover a wonderful truth, in verse 4:

There is forgiveness with you.

Martin Luther, the reformer of Christianity, argued that the 130th Psalm taught the basic truth of the gospel. He preached a sermon on this psalm, and in it he said that in order to amount to something before God, one must rely on grace, not merit.

John Wesley heard Psalm 130 performed as an anthem on May 24, 1738 (that would be 280 years ago) in Saint Paul's Cathedral in London. That same evening he went into a room on Aldersgate Street, and there he experienced the gospel, in which his heart was *strangely warmed* by the grace of God.

I have a friend in another denomination, and a few years ago we were sharing our journeys of ministry in a small group. He told us that he had served a couple of very strong churches, was recognized by his peers. And then he went into a deep depression that lasted a couple of years. He went to a therapist. The therapist urged him to leave the ministry. He found a spiritual director who taught him how to pray the Psalms.

Over time he came to what was, for him, something close to the heart of the problem. He said, "I had turned a religion of grace into a religion of good works and achievement."

J. K. Rowling speaking to a group of really bright students; Martin Luther and John Wesley, scholars who knew a great deal about religion; my friend Tony's testimony. What are they saying to us about failure and imagination?

There seems to be a sort of cottage industry based on the idea that the church has failed, that we as bishops have failed. I am no stranger to the internet!

What is failure?

Failure is the honest scorecard of who we are in relation to God: If you should mark iniquities, Lord, who could stand? It is a rhetorical question, the implied answer being, none of us.

But what if our greatest failure is a failure of imagination?

# 9

# THE DOWNWARD
# MOVEMENT OF GRACE

I think of our church, the Methodist family within the whole body of Christ. Once we were a movement. We moved across England, across the US, across the planet. This was the purpose of the itinerancy. Then, perhaps, over time, we became more rigid, less flexible, more settled, and even stuck. Not speaking about you, just reading some of my own situation!

We began to lose members, many of our sanctuaries became sparsely attended, we closed some of our churches. We did harm to each other as we navigated controversial matters that were and are deeply important. In our prayers of confession, we said these words, "We have failed to be an obedient church." And we needed to say them.

It seemed to be a downward journey, more like wandering in a basement than inhabiting the sanctuary.

What do you do?

It helps to have a scriptural imagination. In the words of Richard Hays, a scriptural imagination is "The capacity to see the world through lenses given to us in Scripture."[1]

We can claim the words of the apostle Paul in Ephesians 3:20: "[God,] who by the power at work within us is able to accomplish abundantly far more than all we can ask or imagine."

We can pray the Psalms, this psalm. It is a psalm that takes us all the

---

1  Richard Hays, "Forming Scriptural Imagination," Panel Discussion at Duke Divinity School, February 11, 2013, https://www.youtube.com/watch?v=hTOVoWbRc0A, at 1:53.

way down, but when you go all the way down, there is a foundation, which
we call grace. At the beginning of our movement there was a foundation.
It was never about being fixed or rigid. Two weeks ago I had the honor of
speaking to the Judicial Council of our church, and a part of that was to
appeal to them to see the relationship between our doctrinal standards and
our theological task.

One of my teachers, Thomas Langford, wrote these words:

> Doctrine reflects the grasp of the church; theology reflects
> the reach of the church. To use another analogy: doctrine is
> the part of the cathedral already completed, exploratory the-
> ology is creative architectural vision and preliminary draw-
> ings for possible new construction.[2]

There is a firm foundation. And that foundation is grace. But grace is
always God's unfinished agenda with us. It was never about our achievement or even good works. It was grace. It requires an imagination to see
this about ourselves and about each other, a scriptural imagination, but it
is there. "I wait for the LORD, my soul waits, / and in his word I hope," the
psalmist continues (v. 5). It is to watch for the morning. It is to believe in
the Resurrection. It is to be a part of the possible new construction.

And, conversely, it means that we have not arrived at closure. I am
drawn again and again in this season to the apostle Paul's words in Ephesians 4, that we bear "with one another in love," that we make "every effort
to maintain the unity of the Spirit in the bond of peace" (vv. 2-3).

Have we arrived at closure on what a way forward looks like? Have we
arrived at closure in the conviction that there is no way forward? Have we
made every effort to maintain the unity of the spirit in the bond of peace?
Have we made every effort?

Do we imagine that God is still able to do something that is beyond
our own human powers?

---

2 Thomas A. Langford, *Doctrine and Theology in The United Methodist Church* (Durham. NC: King-
swood Books, 1991), 204.

To be a people who trust in God is to be a people who have failed, who have sinned, who perhaps have tried as hard as we can and gotten as far as we can in our own strength. Maybe Wesley was there on that Aldersgate evening. Maybe our own denomination, The United Methodist Church, is there in the present moment. Maybe we are there, as leaders, as we sit together in this place.

What do we do?

*De Profundis. Out of the deep we call unto you, O Lord.*

I do not know what is ahead of us, in these next few months. I suspect that you don't know either. Maybe this is our convicted humility.

I do know this. In this psalm there is the good news. Jesus goes to the cross for you and me. He is the Lamb of God who takes upon himself the sin of the world, who cries out to God, on our behalf. It is, in the end, his church and not ours, his body and not ours.

If this is *not* true, none of this matters. If this *is* true, we can make it. God can deliver us out of our present bondage to a new place. I love the words of advice a young person once gave the missionary Vincent J. Donovan:

> Do not try to call them back to where they were, and do not try to call them to where you are, as beautiful as that place might seem to you. You must have the courage to go with them to a place that neither you nor they have ever been before.[3]

And so we lead with a scriptural imagination. We become, once again, a movement. In our failure and our need, we discover again that this is who we are. We lead the church, once again, to trust in God.

To paraphrase the words of Charles Wesley, an echo of Psalm 130:

> Out of the deep, regard our cries
> The fallen raise, the mourners cheer

---

3 Vincent J. Donovan, *Christianity Rediscovered* (Ossining, NY: Orbis Books, 2003), xiii.

O Sun of Righteousness arise
And scatter all our doubt and fear.

Sisters and Brothers, there is a way forward. There is a future with
hope. Let's go there.


Amen.

# 10

# A PEACEABLE KINGDOM CHRISTMAS

A s we approached Advent and Christmas in 2018, there were signs of hope. Our sisters and brothers in the Alabama-West Florida Conference had experienced the devastation of Hurricane Michael in the panhandle in September. We had invited our churches to receive an offering for them. The people of First UMC in Ormond Beach challenged us with a $500,000 matching gift. I was overjoyed to announce that our people had contributed an additional $887,383 toward the needs of our brothers and sisters in the panhandle.

We also received approval for the establishment of a United Methodist Church in the Lowell Correctional Institution, located in the community of Reddick, Florida. Lowell houses more than 2,300 women and is considered to be the largest female prison in the United States. I could envision the lives of women being blessed by the gifts of Christian fellowship and worship and the presence of a pastor who would be a sign of the Good Shepherd's love for them.

In my role as president of the Council of Bishops, I shared a Christmas letter to our global church entitled "A Peaceable Kingdom in a Divided World."

Drawing from the prophecies of Isaiah in the eleventh and sixty-fifth chapters, I had preached a variation on this passage in a number of churches—Christ Fort Lauderdale, St. Timothy's in Greensboro, North

Carolina, Lakeside Fellowship in Sanford, St. John's in Winter Haven, and the First United Methodist Churches in Naples, Lake Wales, and Orlando. I had also been asked to preach to the Florida Southern College community following the election of Donald Trump as president, and I had drawn on this text.

In writing to a twelve-million-member denomination on four continents, I sensed that we also needed the peace of Christ in this season. In two shorts months we would gather in St. Louis for a special session of the General Conference.

Living eight centuries before Christ, the prophet Isaiah had a vision, which over time was given a name: *the peaceable kingdom*. It's a compelling vision: a shoot will come from a stump. A stump is a tree that has been cut down and destroyed. But the hope is that life would come out of destruction. We often place our hopes on a new leader, and so an ideal king would be enthroned and would come from the family of David. A new political order would fulfill the hopes of the people. Historically, this passage may have been read at the coronation of a new king of Judah, with the prayer that the Spirit of the Lord would guide and govern the leader.

Then Isaiah's vision shifts from political science to art, to the creation, a vision of a new heaven and a new earth: the wolf and the lamb will lie down together; no one shall hurt or destroy on God's holy mountain. Paradise will be restored. All nature will sing in harmony. Isaiah is painting a picture: *This is what peace looks like*. This is the peaceable kingdom.

In The United Methodist Church we have reflected on what it means to have a *heart of war* and a *heart of peace*. In seeking a way forward, we have been honest about the ways we have seen each other as issues to be discussed, problems to be solved, and obstacles to be overcome. And we have seen the image of God in each other and listened with empathy to one another. We know what violence looks like, the harm we do to one another, and the harm that we experience.

The prophet asks a different question: "What does peace look like?" This vision of the prophet Isaiah has always been inspirational. You can see it, and, of course, that is a part of what makes it so compelling. In the

1820s, almost two hundred years ago, there was a deep separation within the Quakers living in the United States over slavery. It was a church fight. Some of us have been through church fights. Conflict is present in many of our local churches, in many of our communities, in our nations, and in our global denomination. There are *deep divisions* within the people called Methodist as the year 2018 concludes, over our polity in relation to the LBGTQ community and the interpretation of Scripture.

## THE PAINTER

Edward Hicks lived in Bucks County, Pennsylvania, and was a Quaker minister. To make extra income he painted, mostly responding to the needs of others. He painted tavern signs, farm equipment, whatever was needed, and he was good at it. Although he was self-taught, he had a gift. He began to make a fair amount of money, and this upset his Quaker congregation, who felt that he was violating their customs of simple living. Finally, he became enmeshed in a church split, between those who wanted to live more frugally and others who did not see a problem. He gave up painting and took up farming, but he was a terrible farmer. Later he gave up the preaching ministry, too, and transitioned back to the craft of painting.

Soon enough, he came to discover that he could use his painting to express his faith. He began to draw oil paintings based on Isaiah's prophecy: The wolf shall live with the lamb, a little child shall lead them (11:6). He drew the same painting over and over again, and there are now over one hundred versions. We know it now as the *Peaceable Kingdom*, and it is his best-known work. One version of the painting is in the Metropolitan Museum of Art in New York City; another is in the National Gallery of Art in Washington DC; another, which inspired the composer Randall Thompson, is in the Worchester Art Museum in Massachusetts; and, another is in the Reynolda House, a few miles away from one of the congregations my wife, Pam, and I served, in Winston-Salem, North Carolina.

In most of the paintings the predators and prey are together. There is a bull, a lion, a lamb, a bear, a child. They are most often to the right of the painting, congested together. For the artist the animals reflected something of our temperaments—the lion was anger, the bear was calmness. To the left there is often a separate scene, William Penn conducting a treaty with native Americans, the first peoples. A river flows toward them, and light shines upon them. The Spirit, the light placed within us by God, helps us dwell together in peace, despite our animosities and our differences.

It could be that Edward Hicks was inspired to paint this picture, over and over again, because he was obsessed with a vision of peace. Perhaps it was due to the growing division in America between North and South over the practice of slavery. Perhaps it was due to the conflict that was present in his own community, over the teachings of his church and his lifestyle. Perhaps it was due to the inner turmoil within, over what exactly God wanted him to do with his life.

## THE THEOLOGIAN

As I was graduating from divinity school, Stanley Hauerwas published a book entitled *The Peaceable Kingdom*. His earlier works had been collections of essays in the field of Christian ethics; this was an attempt to write an introduction to his discipline, from the perspective of character, virtue, and narrative. The title was taken from Isaiah's prophecy and the introduction included a discussion of the painting of Edward Hicks. In time, Hauerwas would become one of our most influential theologians.

In *The Peaceable Kingdom*[1], Hauerwas suggests that Christians are called to bear witness to the truth of the Holy Scriptures, noting that "this world is the creation of a good God who is known through . . . the life, death and resurrection of Jesus" (15). We believe this to be the truth of the gospel, and yet we cannot use violence in the advancement of this truth. Instead we have trust and confidence in the ultimate victory of God over

---

1  Stanley Hauerwas, *The Peaceable Kingdom: A Primer in Christian Ethics* (Notre Dame, IN: University of Notre Dame Press, 1983), page numbers noted within parentheses in text.

the forces of evil, sin, and death. In a fragmented and polarized world, this is crucial: Christians with liberal and conservative convictions are tempted to use coercive strategies for the sake of an end they believe to be just, and Christian leaders mimic the practices of our secular counterparts in seeking strategic gains through actions that are not consistent with our covenant promises.

At our best, we understand that leaders never cease being disciples. The formation of character and conscience takes place through immersion into the Christian narrative and participation in the Christian community. We discover that we are sinners, that we have a continuing capacity for self-deception. To be a Christ-follower is to move beyond individualism to see the persons God has called us to serve; in so doing we discover the needs of others to be the pathways to our freedom, as they remove the greatest obstacle to freedom, namely our self-absorption (44).

Freed from self-absorption, as individuals and congregations, we are given new life. The call of God is, in Hauerwas's words, "the confidence, gained through participation in . . . God's kingdom, to trust ourselves and others. . . . Such confidence becomes the source of our character and our freedom as we are loosed from a debilitating preoccupation with ourselves" (49).

## THE PRESENT MOMENT

United Methodism, at the conclusion of 2018, had become a church infected by "a debilitating preoccupation with ourselves." Many of our congregations do not have the energy or will to be in mission beyond the walls of the sanctuary. Commenting a few days after his election to the papacy, Pope Francis spoke of the "self-referential church," which believes that "she has her own light," and "lives to give glory only to one another, and not the rest of the world." At a denominational and structural level, we in The UMC often reflect the systemic polarization of our political cultures; our social pronouncements, even those that advance values of inclusion, protection of the vulnerable, and seek peace, are often harsh and brittle. Ironically, these pronouncements become louder as the church itself becomes more marginalized, fragmented, and disconnected from the real world.

Our fragmentation, violence, and disconnection are signs that "we have failed to be an obedient church," in the language of our prayer of confession (*The United Methodist Hymnal*, p. 8). In our individual lives, in our congregations, in the Council of Bishops, in our denomination, in our nation, we yearn for a right path, for a new and living way, for an alternative to the status quo. In the language of the hymn, there are "fightings and fears within, without" (*The United Methodist Hymnal*, 357, stanza 3).

The way forward may be the rediscovery of our core mission: "to make disciples of Jesus Christ, for the transformation of the world" (*The Book of Discipline*, 2016; ¶120). Jesus is the embodiment of the peaceable kingdom. To recall the words of the Gospel about John the Baptist: "he himself was not the light, but he came to testify to the light" (John 1:8). The church approximates the peaceable kingdom as she stays close to the person and work of Christ. This is an act of radical self-denial. The first task of a disciple, Hauerwas notes, is not to forgive, but to learn to be forgiven (89). To confess our need for forgiveness is an act of humility, and one that calls upon the patience of God. To confess that we need to be forgiven is to give up control and to place ourselves in communion with God's people, who are also imperfect and, yet, who are God's chosen messengers of grace and acceptance for us.

## THE QUESTION

And so we gather under the cross and flame, in communities around the world, to discover anew the meaning and message of Advent and Christmas. As United Methodists, the words of an eighth-century BC prophet, the vision of an eighteenth-century painter, and the writings of a twentieth-century theologian can guide us, for our questions and struggles remain the same:

How do we discover restored relationships?

Why is it so difficult for us to ask for forgiveness?

How do we most faithfully advocate for those who have been treated unjustly?

How do we accept God's will for the future?

Where do we find the capacity to live in fellowship with those who differ from us?

What is our vision of peace?

The ruins and devastation surround the prophet Isaiah in the eighth-century BC, but he remains faithful: he sits still long enough, listens closely enough, discerns carefully enough, and it becomes clear. God paints a picture for him, and us. It is a portrait of anger and calmness, strength and weakness, living together. Could this vision exist, in the present moment: in our nations, in our denomination, in our local churches, in our families, within each of us?

Perhaps, in the words of Hauerwas, "we have the grace to do one thing" (149–151), meaning we live in community, we stay in connection and we engage in the basic practices of discipleship that make the forgiveness and love of God visible and tangible. This is the peaceable kingdom. And so I wondered:

How can The United Methodist Church, in its global expression, become a sign of this peaceable kingdom?

# 11

# THE HARD WORK OF LISTENING

Some of the tensions in our church—and here I am speaking of the inner core of leadership, where the engagement is most intense—can be ascribed to real differences in the history of Christian spirituality. The dark side of holiness and justice movements can be an excessive judgment of culture and focus on right actions. The Reformed tradition, in which a few of our leaders have been shaped, is an emptying (apophatic) form of spirituality that is also more about thinking than feeling. Wesleyan tradition differs in that it tends to the affect (experiential) and is more relational and more engaging with the world (cataphatic or positive).

I realize this is complex and conceptually this is not for everyone. But the history of Christian spirituality and theology is deep, rich, and complex. It is not simple or simplistic. Most of us resonate with one part of the Christian tradition, but the danger is seeing that corner of the world as the fullness of God's intention for faithfulness. This is never the case.

The truth is in the whole.

I have learned, in twenty-eight years as a pastor and in seven years as a bishop, that there is a basic goodness in people. It is rooted in the image of God.

Along the way we do get damaged by the ways we have been harmed. Sometimes we fix blame on a person or group. We may be reading the situation accurately. And, at times, we may be very wrong.

We are naturally drawn to those who confirm our suspicions or opinions. Sometimes we call these tribes or political parties or life groups or denominations.

We should not be too hard on ourselves for seeking out these enclaves. Sometimes we need the security, the agreement, the amen to whatever we have just said or done.

We need these enclaves, but they can also contribute to the harm. If you have ever been a part of the tribe and find yourself for some reason outside of the tribe, you understand.

So, the calling is to see the good in someone outside your political party, your tribe, your self-identification. It is a call to maturity, to growth, to becoming unstuck.

I'm not asking you to leave it. Simply to see the good in someone very unlike you. The image of God is there, waiting to be rediscovered.

In the other person, and in us.

For me, it has always been about the power of listening (see Dietrich Bonhoeffer, *Life Together*, a small classic that anyone in a local church could read), and the liberation people experience when they are seen and heard and feel accepted and loved. Many are looking for a friendship like that or a church like that or a pastor like that. Or a gospel like that.

I do believe some of our differences will lessen over the next ten years. Church will be harder to do. Christians will feel they are more in the minority. People will figure out what they need from a denomination and what they don't. But what they need, they will need.

The effect of four years of a Trump presidency will create a need for the rebuilding of an evangelical movement after the fact. This is difficult to work out now, as many established ties among leaders and donors and friends are strong and people understandably do not want to be cast out or to sever these relationships. Empathy often trumps purpose.

At the same time, progressives desperately need the gifts many evangelicals have—a strong faith and trust, a hopefulness about the church and leaders even when they have been betrayed, and even when that betrayal has come from evangelical leaders. Most of all progressives can learn from evangelicals of the necessity that we must reproduce, be born again, give birth to movements, disciple younger generations and be (reverse) mentored. There is no future progressive movement without an evangelical soul.

And yes, right now the political toxicity makes this almost impossible to live out or even see or trust.

So to bring very different people together to listen and to speak the truth we know only in part and to be a part of the body of Christ that seeks unity without uniformity (I know that sounds like a cliché—but, be honest, in your uniqueness there is some part of you that appreciates this!) is a worthy calling.

It would be easy not to do this work. It is a worthy calling.

Margaret Wheatley has said that conversation is the currency of change. We do need change. The change may tear us apart—internally. This is *metanoia* (repentance). It may leave us in fragments. But if we have learned the tools of civil conversation, Fresh Expressions, and design thinking, and I would add Greg Ellison's model of Fearless Dialogues and Gary Mason's work with Re-Thinking Conflict, God can do something with us. I imagine this has already started to happen.

As 2018 turned to 2019, with a momentous General Conference less than two months ahead, I found myself grateful for disciples of Jesus who are willing to lean into this difficult, even courageous conversation. For every person who left the table, I am convinced that someone else hears the still, small voice. And I remain convinced that we need more, not less, of these conversations in the years ahead.

# 12

# AN EPIPHANY MIDRASH

The Scriptures for Epiphany—especially Isaiah 60 and Matthew 2—confirm what I sensed in twenty-eight years of pastoral ministry: the light is not confined to the candles we lift up in our sanctuaries, and the desire to offer gifts is not limited to our church members. Both passages of Scripture widen our angle of vision to include those outside our ethnic groups and tribes. The beauty of the gospel is that it always breaks apart our inclination to limit what God can do and who God can use.

The purpose of the church is to tell this story, to keep this flame alive, to see the potential for good in all people. Surely this is the thrust of Isaiah 40–66. Surely this is at the heart of why Jesus himself resonated with the prophet Isaiah and perceived his mission in these chapters. One cannot read Isaiah 49:6 apart from Matthew 28:19-20. And one cannot read the Gospels without seeing how they (and especially Luke) flow into Acts, and how what had been unclean is made clean.

For a time, God will allow us the luxury of being shaped by the culture wars and partisan political preferences of our nation-state. And for a time, God will allow us our political and sociological languages to tell some version, however inadequate, of our stories. But a generation will arise who will return to the sources that give life, the deep tradition of Scripture that includes the outsider in every conceivable way, that honors the search, that accepts every sacrifice.

This generation will purge itself of our tribalism, which I take to be Isaiah's big idea. And the revelation, the manifestation of glory, the epiphany will be given to the unlikeliest among us. What began in a small village (Bethlehem) was never intended to remain there. It would rock the world, even of Herod.

## AN UNEXPECTED PHONE CALL

As 2019 began, Pam and I flew to Miami, where we drove with Cynthia Weems, the superintendent, to the Key West United Methodist Church. I would preach at their 175th anniversary.

As we were driving out of the Keys, my sister called with the news that my mother was not well. I had been invited to speak with the North Texas Conference clergy about the Way Forward over the next two days. My friend Mike McKee was very understanding. I was able to change my schedule and stopped instead in Atlanta and drove to Columbus, Georgia, where she lives. I went directly to St. Francis Hospital, where she was in congestive heart failure.

The next few days were intense, visiting with my mother, alongside my sister and brother. It felt very healthy to reconnect and I knew I was in the right place. I was able to cancel a number of things on my schedule, including an ecumenical service, a preaching appointment, and a conference at St. Simon's Island. At the end of the week, on Sunday evening, Pam and I prepared to join many from Florida at St. Simons, where we would be led by Tod Bolsinger.

My mother was stable, although very ill. I had good conversations with my brother and sister. Our daughters had also joined us. I prayed with my mother and gave thanks for her. And then Pam and I drove across the state, from west to the east coast of Georgia.

About forty-five minutes from Epworth By The Sea, we received a call that we needed to return, and so we did.

The next morning, my mother began the process of dying. We were all there, and it was a gift to be able to hold her hand as she labored over her last breaths. I remembered that this was the same hospital, St. Francis, in which she had given birth to me.

Life does come full circle.

## MY MOTHER'S DEATH

A few days later I would give her eulogy, at her home church, Mt. Zion, and I shared some of her story. My mother gave birth to me when she was a teenager. She graduated from high school in June and I was born in August. I am aware that my life was made possible because of her sacrifices, and I imagine the postponement of many of her dreams. She provided for us, she protected us, she loved us, she was the one who held our families together.

She was creative and artistic. I remember the pride I felt when our family would be at Pritchett's Fish Camp, waiting for a table, and my mother's mural was hanging in the waiting area. I remembered her painting it, and I wanted to go up to the strangers around us and say, "My mother painted that mural!" She was gifted.

My mother had two extraordinary parents, Bill and Bernice, Gran-Gran and Nannie. I know the difference between parents, who discipline, and the grandparents, who are all about unconditional love. But there was a lot of both of them in my mother. She gave that love to her two families, in succession. She attended to the everyday needs and activities of Jeremy, her son who was born with Down syndrome. They loved the Springer Opera House, where they volunteered and attended plays.

She was an educator. And she was an excellent teacher. She was the kind of teacher you hope and pray for in your child's experience. She was named as teacher of the year in the Muscogee County School District, the first to be given that honor. I remember in the summer she took classes to get better at her profession. She earned degrees from Auburn and Columbus State. And I also remember overhearing her, in the evening, calling parents and the message would be something like this: "I am calling to let you know that Johnny is failing my class and we have a test tomorrow and I hope he can study because we want him to pass!"

Over the years I would give my mother copies of books I had written and she would read them. Once I was asked to write notes for the Wesley Study Bible. These are the words that are printed on the bottom of a page, that explain a verse or place a verse in context with another verse or in relation to a doctrine. When we saw each other, I gave her a copy and she had a quizzical look on her face, as if to say, on the one hand, "I am proud of you," and on the other, "You are the boy and teenager I watched grow up and you are writing in a Bible?"

I explained to her that the words in study Bibles are not the Bible. They are written by ordinary people. And that is who we were and are. We are ordinary people, saints and sinners. We have the treasure of the gospel in earthen vessels, the apostle Paul wrote in 2 Corinthians, to show that the power belongs to God and not to us.

Being in this sanctuary reminded me of the generations of our family, worshipping there, and sitting between my mother and my grandfather in worship as a child and how good that felt. My grandfather would bring paper to write on, because it would be bad stewardship to draw on the envelopes, and so he and I would draw animals.

## A SEARCH FOR PEACE

A story about my grandfather. He was a Quaker, and that meant he was a conscientious objector during World War II. I remember seeing him read the Quaker pamphlets. During my ruptured quad tendon rehab my mother sent me a box of letters and postcards her parents and grandparents had sent to each other.

In one of them, my great-grandfather, Grampa, was writing to the head of the Quaker church in Philadelphia. It was a one-page letter but he was in essence asking one question: Can my son be a Quaker if there are no Quaker churches around him?

The Quaker official wrote back, again the response was about one page long, and the basic response was "Yes, he can." And then he wrote, "If you will give me his address, I will stop by and visit him on my way to Florida." Gran-Gran was a person of peace. For him that meant working in the shipyards of Mobile during the war as his form of service.

This was the same peace we wanted and needed that day. It is the same peace I wanted and needed when I walked down aisle of this same church and made a public profession of faith in Jesus Christ.

It is the same peace I believe my mother received when she took her last breath on that Monday morning. Her physical body had reached its limit. But there was and is God's peace, which surpasses human understanding.

And through it all, I continue to search for that peace.

# 13

# FEBRUARY 2019, ST. LOUIS, PART 1

The year 2018 had flowed into 2019, in some ways it was something of a blur, and we were in St. Louis, at the called Special Session of the General Conference.

I took a moment to catch my breath. Over the past few months I had spoken at the memorial service of one of my very closest friends from divinity school, Skip Parvin. I had met with members of the Florida Conference who identified with the Wesleyan Covenant Association over an extended lunch. I had spoken at town hall meetings in several cities across the annual conference and had responded to questions and comments during the meetings. I had been privileged to share a meal and listen to two profound theologians, Jurgen Moltmann and Miroslav Volf, on the campus of our neighboring Florida Southern College where I have taught and served as a trustee. My wife, Pam, had preached at Hyde Park UMC in Tampa, sharing some of the remarkable story of her life with the Haitian people which predated our time in Florida.

Gil Rendle had led a Christmas retreat for our cabinet on quietly courageous leadership. Alice Williams and Debby Zutter had hosted a group of us at the Disney Candlelight Service, an annual lessons and carols service held at Epcot. There is always a celebrity narrator, and this evening it had been Cal Ripken, the baseball legend!

The year had begun with our weekend preaching in the Florida Keys and then the unexpected death of my mother. The correspondence leading to the impending gathering in St. Louis became heavier and more intense.

I could also sense rising anxiety levels among the clergy and laity across Florida. I had been working with a coach, which involved a conversation about every six to eight weeks. She knew my experience of grief, and the intensity of the coming General Conference, so she encouraged me to place a couple of fun and unrelated dates on my calendar.

So I flew across the country to see our older daughter who was in graduate studies at UCLA. We attended a basketball game at Pauley Pavilion, one of the iconic sports venues in the world. On the way back, I stopped in Nashville where I got to hang out for a day with our granddaughter!

These were life-giving experiences—a reminder to me that I was more than my role. Then I preached on Sunday in Fort Meade, Florida, followed by appointment-making with our district superintendents, and mediating a complaint process toward a just resolution. Finally, I packed, and Pam and I flew to St. Louis.

In the office of bishop I receive a steady stream of letters questioning Scripture and our welcome of the LGBTQ community.

I have received some feedback questioning the terms "wideness" and "generous" and the need for them.

I respect this feedback. A first simple response:

Some do want to be in the church—they want to live and grow in their faith—and they find themselves on the shadow side of orthodoxy . . . no longer accepted in the church, for some reason.

The wideness in God's mercy reminds us of the waiting parent in the parable of the prodigal son, or the hymn "Amazing Grace." When we are orthodox in our belief, we discover a God who is generous toward us, in the gift of salvation. And when we are orthodox in our living, we are generous toward each other. We forgive, because we have been forgiven. We give, because we have first received.

As I approached the Special Session, this became my prayer:

> O God, I thank you for the life you have given to me.
>
> Where I have not seen all of this as your gift,
> forgive me.

2016     2017     2018     2019     2020

Where I have insisted on privilege and preference,
   have mercy on me.
Where I have dwelled on real or perceived harms,
   grant me your peace.

Teach me to meditate
   on the wideness of your mercy.
Teach me to reflect
   on the vastness of your patience.
Teach me to depend
   on the miracle of your grace.

I am finally accountable to you for this life.
And your judgment of me
will have less to do with where I stand,
and more to do with how I saw and welcomed you
in the broken, the powerless, and the vulnerable.

You were, and are, always there.

And so you continue to call me to follow,
   to let go of many things,
      and to cast my net in deeper waters.

You are faithful, O God. I trust you. Amen.

# 14

# FEBRUARY 2019, ST. LOUIS, PART 2

On the Friday before General Conference in February, I gave a reflection to the Council of Bishops on regulating our anxiety and understanding the stress across the church. Years ago I had the blessing of studying for a year with Ed Friedman, the family systems theorist. Friedman wrote,

> The overall health and functioning of any organization depend primarily on one or two people at the top, and . . . this is true whether the relationship system is a personal family, a sports team, an orchestra, a congregation, a religious hierarchy, or an entire nation."[1]

In a season of stress we are called to pursue self-differentiation. Self-differentiation is the capacity of the leader to discern his or her clear position, to be able to state this clearly, and to stay in touch with others in the system (not withdraw). A self-differentiated person knows where she ends and where others begin—she is not fused with them. Self-differentiation is more helpful than charisma or consensus.

To the degree that we are not dependent on the praise or even support of the relationship system, we can become more detached, even as we are present. To the extent that the leader can become detached, he makes the field less anxious and promotes creativity. In healthier systems there is a

---

1 Edwin H. Friedman, *Generation to Generation: Family Process in Church and Synagogue* (NY: Guilford Press, 2011), 221.

greater range of responses to the stress. When the anxiety level is high, the system is more reactive and less thoughtful. When the anxiety level is lowered, the system becomes more thoughtful.

The bishops are called to claim a vision for the church; to make disciples of Jesus; to speak prophetically, which connects the gospel with alleviating human suffering; and to be passionate about the unity of the church (*The Book of Discipline*, 2016; ¶403).

I knew that we would exercise this calling in the coming days primarily through conversations, honoring people across their differences, and presiding in a way that upholds the values of fairness and equality. The 864 delegates who are arriving from across the world would deliberate, discern, and act. The work was in their hands. My fellow bishops and I were there to support them.

I had been interviewed by the *New York Times*, the *Washington Post*, the *Wall Street Journal*, Associated Press, *USA Today*, and NPR in the weeks leading up to General Conference. The headlines were often inflammatory, and I had no control over the others who were interviewed. I attempted to talk about who we are as a global church, how the decision would affect people in the pews, and how the decisions would be made.

Before General Conference began, the Commission on a Way Forward had dinner with the Council of Bishops. It was a gift to introduce these thirty-two persons to the bishops, and for the bishops to hear their voices. It was a gift to offer words of gratitude for them, along with colleague moderators Sandra Steiner Ball and David Yemba.

On February 23, 2019, we spent a day in prayer for the upcoming Special Session, which would begin the next day. I recall . . .

- Being prayed over, with laying on of hands, by Bishops Martinez, Galvan, and Ortiz (of Puerto Rico), as the "*presidente obispo*."
- Seeing a number of longtime friends, including Sky McCracken, my prayer partner on the jurisdictional committee on episcopacy.
- Lunch with Janice Huie and Robert Schnase and dinner with Will Willimon. I have learned so much from each of them.

- Anointing a number of people with oil for healing.
- One requested healing for harm done to gay and lesbian persons in his family. Another healing of memories.
- A woman requested healing in the return of her cancer. One requested healing for the church.
- Requesting forgiveness from each other. I made this request of Woodie White, who has also taught me so much and has been a constant encourager.
- Seeing most of the Florida delegates.
- A conversation with Sue Haupert-Johnson about what all of this means to many people who are not in church, or not yet in church.
- A conversation with Mike Lowry about the church in Africa, and with Jim Sallley about Africa University.
- The honor of being one of the celebrants in the service of Holy Communion.

# PRAYER FOR FAITHFULNESS, FRUITFULNESS, AND UNITY

*On February 25, the second day of the 2019 General Conference, this prayer that I had written two years earlier was on my heart, and I shared it with the Florida Annual Conference back home.*

O God whose nature and name is love:
We pray for the light that shines in the darkness, the radiant light that we see in the face of Jesus Christ our Lord and Savior. Give us the faith to grow into his likeness, and give us the confidence to follow him.

We pray for the faithfulness of the church—that we would walk in your ways, trusting in your providence, listening for your voice.

We pray for the fruitfulness of the church—that we would make new disciples of Jesus Christ, in new places and in new ways, for the transformation of the world.

And we pray for the unity of the church—that we would live with a heart of peace and insofar as it depends on us, that we would seek to live in peace with all people.

May the work that has been done by the Commission on a Way Forward and the Council of Bishops, and is now in the hands of the General Conference, be a living sacrifice, holy and acceptable to you.

And may we, the people of The United Methodist Church, more fully offer to the world the grace that we have received, the grace that has brought us safe thus far, and the grace that will lead us home.

In the name of Jesus, our teacher and healer and for the sake of his body, the church. Amen.

# 15

# FEBRUARY 2019, ST. LOUIS, PART 3

We gathered in St. Louis to discern a way forward for our beloved church. We brought with us enough luggage for a few days, and a few other essential items. If people were like me they brought with them some measure of anxiety and yet also the assurance that many were praying for them. We came here from the north and the south and the east and the west.

And we each came to this moment with a story. It could be a story of pain or hope. It could be the story of our salvation, or how God has used us to offer Christ to others, or how we have been a reconciling person in our community. It could be the story of an opportunity that God made possible for us, through this church.

If we look around, and reflect for a moment, it will occur to us that ours is not the only story. My story is not the only story. Your story is not the only story. So, we sit in these places, these privileged places, to share our stories and to listen to the stories of others.

The good news is that God has a story too. I want to enter into God's story through the language of the apostle Paul. It is a story of divided peoples, and the power of God to include what we have excluded, to make clean what we have called profane, to salvage what we have discarded.

It is a creation story. We think we are here to divide something, or to dismantle something. That may be our story. God's story is about creation, a new humanity and making peace and breaking down the dividing wall of hostility that is between us.

We can be honest. We come to this in our divisions. Our languages divide us. Our life experiences divide us. Our opinions divide us.

Over the three years between the 2016 General Conference in Portland and the 2019 General Conference in St. Louis, I was asked by the church to watch and listen. To watch and listen for the good in conservatives, progressives, centrists. To hear their testimonies and honor the work of the Holy Spirit in them. To assume the best about them. It was not unlike the work I had done earlier, over twenty-eight years, as a pastor. Some of the most conservative and progressive people in my experience inhabited the churches I served, sang in the same choirs, studied the Bible together, spent the night with the homeless, mentored youth.

I learned to watch and listen for the faith underneath the surface. It motivated them to be in those local churches and, yes, to be United Methodists.

I learned to watch and listen for the connections between them. When illness or death came, they prayed for each other. When an economic crisis crippled a city, they wrote checks and collected food. When they disagreed about how to interpret Scripture, they imagined they were still learning and growing as disciples and had not arrived.

The Commission on a Way Forward was a process of watching and listening. It was not an interruption to the work of God. It was and is the work. It was not an argument that distracted us from the mission. It was and is the mission. In February 2019, the work and the mission were in the hands of the delegates to General Conference.

If you watch and listen for the good in conservatives, centrists, and progressives, you will see the cross and the flame. You will see people carrying the cross. You will see people who are living the prayer, "kindle in us the fire of your love," because the Holy Spirit dwells in them. You will see people loving those who do not love them. In the three days of the 2019 General Conference, we would continue to watch and listen. We would gather under the cross and the flame as people who have professed our faith in Jesus Christ as our Lord and Savior. And we would pray for the gift of the Holy Spirit, to make us one with Christ, one with each other, and one in ministry to all the world.

Make us one!

Unity is for the sake of the mission. Where you see the mission of God, you will see people connected to each other, for this very purpose.

The divisions are easy to see. What would it be like for us to watch and listen for the connections?

What connects us? It is not our stories. It is God's story. We hear a fragment of God's story from the apostle Paul. It helps to remember how radical was his life and ministry.

- Ananias was sent to Paul and embraced him (the enemy) as "brother" (Acts 9).
- Paul remembered his "call" story and constantly shared it (Acts 22).
- Paul followed Jesus, which meant traveling the way of the cross (Galatians 2).
- Paul confessed his sin and struggles (Romans 7).
- Paul was willing to resolve conflict with other leaders, for the sake of the mission (Acts 15; Galatians 1).
- Paul led teams of women and men and developed an understanding of diverse spiritual gifts (Romans 12 and 16; 1 Corinthians 12 and 14).
- Paul planted churches in strategic crossroads where the gospel engaged many diverse cultures (1 and 2 Corinthians; Ephesians).
- Paul was a passionate advocate for the unity of the body of Christ (Ephesians 4).
- Paul knew the difference between church and empire, koinonia and colonialism (Romans 12; Acts 17).

In Paul's writing there is a movement from evangelism to doxology to life together. God overcame the almost insurmountable division between human sinfulness and divine holiness. God overcame these divisions in the New Testament church and united it in mission. God through Christ shows us the way of peace amid our polarizations and binaries.

Because God has done all of this—more than we can ask or imagine—are we bold enough to believe that God could do this again?

It is as if Paul is saying, to the Ephesians, there are these two groups and God abolished the dividing wall of hostility between them, praise God, and now we sing the doxology to this One God, and, . . . God can do it again.

John Wesley wrote, in *The Scripture Way of Salvation*, and I paraphrase:

It is a divine evidence and conviction . . . that what God has promised God is able to perform. We admit that with us it is impossible, to make something clean from the unclean, to purify our hearts from sin, and to till the ground of our hearts with holiness. Yet with God there is no difficulty, since with God all things are possible—If God speaks it, it shall be done. "God said, 'Let there be light,' and there was light" (Genesis 1:3).

God is able.

Think of your own life, your own journey. What God has made possible. How Jesus has walked with you. How the Spirit came like wind or fire or a still small voice. It is your story. It is God's new creation in you.

Say a prayer of thanksgiving in your own heart language, right here, right now, for all that God has done through you. Yes, through it all, there are these dividing walls. We came to St. Louis pretty equally divided. I am no stranger to the speculations or the surveys!

But could these three days be a time when Jesus might reconcile both "groups" (and all our associated tribes) into one body?

And, if I could be permitted to be theological for a moment, could it be that Jesus has already done this? Could it be that Jesus has already broken down the dividing wall of hostility that is between us and made peace through the blood of the cross?

The cross, what God has done for us. And the flame, the fruit of the Holy Spirit, love and joy and peace and patience.

Patience. Evangelism and doxology create something new, and that is a people who are in connection with each other. That is you and me, that's us. That is the people of the cross and the flame.

So we have been called, in humility, which means we allow our story to become a part of God's greater story, and we are gentle with each other, which means we do no harm, because every person with whom you share this space is created in the image of God, and we are patient, we bear with one another in love—that is sanctification—we bear witness to the world that we love each other because God first loved us, and . . . we make every effort to maintain the unity of the Spirit in the bond of peace.

I am convicted by these words from the Rule of Taize:

> Never resign yourself to the scandal of the separation of Christians who so readily profess love for their neighbor, and yet remain divided. Make the unity of the body of Christ your passionate concern.

It is an echo of the Scripture:

> [Make] every effort to maintain the unity of the Spirit in the bond of peace (Ephesians 4:3).

And this leads to a series of uncomfortable questions. Have we made every effort? Can we allow our stories to become a part of a much bigger story? What if we imagined that this means more to God than it does to us? What if, in our life together, we became an outward and visible sign of the cross and the flame?

What if we sought to hold together an evangelical orthodoxy with a radical hospitality to all people and trusted that God will journey with them (and us) toward a holiness that is not ours to define in this life?

What if we admitted that, in a post-Christian culture, when we speak of holiness the world hears judgment? What if holiness is experienced in the unexpected encounter with God (Isaiah 6) and in small circles of trust with each other, which we once called class and band meetings, or, to coin a phrase, "Christian conferencing"?

2016    2017    2018    2019    2020

What if separation is never the path to holiness, division is never the way to revival, and schism is never an expression of the One Body?

What if searching for the exits is easier but less faithful, more aligned with our preferences but less reflective of the One who never gives up on us?

What if there is a deep center and a great tradition worth claiming? We know how to sing this, and it is about the very nature of God.

"So free, so infinite his grace! Tis mercy all, immense and free." "Jesus thou art all compassion; pure, unbounded love thou art!"

What if, like our Lord, we were to "empty ourselves of all but love"?

Sisters and brothers, in these three days, make every effort to maintain the unity of the Spirit in the bond of peace. Make the unity of the body of Christ your passionate concern. Remember: you are the people of the cross and the flame.

Imagine that you and I are still learning and growing as disciples and we have not arrived, and so we say, in these days, "Finish then, thy new creation"!

Sisters and brothers what if God is able to do abundantly more than we can ask or imagine?

Hear the good news:

What God has promised he is able to perform. God is able!

Amen.

*Book Three*

# God Will Make a Way

2019-2020

# LETTER TO THE FLORIDA ANNUAL CONFERENCE

*After the decision by the 2019 General Conference to affirm the Traditional Plan, I sent this letter to the Florida Annual Conference.*

Dear Florida Brothers and Sisters in Christ,

Some are grateful for the results of the Special Session. And others sought a different outcome. All of this will take some time to process. Human sexuality is a topic on which our people have differing views. As evidenced by the vote of the Special Session, we are a global church with very different contexts. We were not able to achieve contextual differentiation as envisioned by the Commission on a Way Forward. By a majority vote, we passed the Traditional Plan, with some parts ruled unconstitutional. It now goes to the Judicial Council for review at their next meeting, but our existing *Discipline* language is maintained.

We are a global church. This is a great gift in that God blesses us with diversity and the gospel is lived and shared across cultures. This is a great challenge in that we have different understandings of the LGBTQ community and, indeed, the LGBTQ persons in our own churches.

By a majority, the US church seems to favor the One Church Plan that would have more openly welcomed pastors from the LGBTQ community and allowed for same-sex marriage. And an overwhelming majority of the Council of Bishops endorsed the One Church Plan.

I am a person of evangelical and orthodox faith and respect those who see this primarily as a matter of scriptural interpretation. I will continue to live my promises of consecration as a bishop by abiding by *The Book of Discipline* as a resource for oversight and supervision in support of the church's mission (*BOD*, 2016; ¶403).

Some believe the arc of history is moving toward more acceptance of LGBTQ people, not less. Pew Research teaches us that younger generations in the US, especially under forty-five and more so under thirty, will not participate in a church that rejects the LGBTQ community. A letter from United Methodists under the age of thirty-five was shared at the Special Session, with over 15,500 signatories. A greater number of LGBTQ voices were heard on the floor of the Special Session than ever before. Many of these were younger voices.

I offer the following words to the LGBTQ community:

> Please know that you are of sacred worth. You are not the problem. You are not "out there." You are present in our churches. You bless us with your faith and your gifts strengthen the church. And my calling, for you and all people, is to remove the obstacles to your experience of the grace of God, and especially in the life of The United Methodist Church.

I also offer these words to the evangelical community:

> Please know that your faith is a great gift to God and to your local churches. Too often, your stances have been misunderstood as driven by hatred, as opposed to being of deeply held faith. Your lives have been changed by the good news of Jesus, and you have a deep desire that others know this grace. Our denomination is blessed by you and needs your gifts in our calling to share God's love across the world. Our conference includes at every level of leadership evangelicals who are of the utmost integrity.

We remain a denomination that is open to people of all nations, ethnic groups, ages, and sexual orientations. We hope to find better ways to embrace our diversity and be on mission together.

Despite our differences, we will continue to work together to make disciples of Jesus Christ for the transformation of the world and to share God's love with all people.

⁓

*Shortly after I returned to Florida, I shared this message with the conference:*

I remember years ago hearing a recording of Henri Nouwen. He was seated at a dinner party next to a wealthy woman who talked at length about the failures of the Catholic Church and the church's rejection of her.

At some point Nouwen was moved to say, directly to her, "I hear you. I do. But I want you to hear this as well. I am the Catholic Church. I do not reject you. Every day I want to be in the presence of Jesus. I want you to know that you are always in the presence of Jesus. And he does not reject you. He loves you. And in his name I love you. And that is the Catholic Church."

I am back home in Florida. And now I need to embody the grace and love of Jesus for people in direct ways. What the church's language cannot say, I need to live. Finally, we have more than enough words.

People really want to know that we love them. And if we speak for or represent the church, this will help them to take a small step toward trusting that Jesus loves them.

This is my work. Pray for me.

# 1

# A LENTEN SEASON

Ash Wednesday reminds me of my mortality and finitude. There were certainly experiences of that over the months before and after the 2019 General Conference—the deaths of two close friends from divinity school, Skip Parvin and Elizabeth Graves, and then of my mother. And the death, after our time in St. Louis, of a form of unity that would have given a greater role for conscience across our diverse church and a greater acceptance of all people. And here I am not talking about a particular plan or petition.

As a pastor I have tried to give others permission to grieve. I've not always been so good at that myself. My life of privilege has in many ways been an ever-widening experience of opportunity and possibility. I have been and remain surrounded by abundance in most every way. I can count these many blessings and name them one by one.

But having the ashes imposed on my forehead on Ash Wednesday and reading Psalm 51 remind me of limitations that are real. The most significant limitation may be my lack of faith. All of this teaches me to return, again and again, to the mercy of the One who created me from the dust.

The forty days of Lent in the wake of the 2019 General Conference were, as they always are, a time to grieve. Not to blame. Not to have someone else's experience. Not to assume a righteousness that is greater than another. Not to wallow in self-pity. And not to be a people-pleaser.

But to appropriately name losses, and, over time, to turn and return to what is life-giving. Because each of those forty days is a step closer to something new.

The stone will be rolled away.

The tomb will be empty.

And the spirit will be poured out on all flesh.

On the first Friday in Lent, it is the tradition of the church to focus on the cross and to read Psalm 51. Without a deep and constant turning to Jesus, we are always prone to pride and arrogance, we are always tempted by power and using any means to achieve our ends, even those we believe to be of God.

A church that loses touch with the spiritual practice of focusing on the cross and reading Psalm 51 will inevitably transfer its trust to institutions and leaders who are always in need of reform and renewal.

To read Psalm 51 is to be utterly transparent and open to the truth—in our spiritual lives and in our institutional practices. This leads us—as persons before God and as leaders of communities—to a deep and constant dependence on God, who has the power to change us, who is finally the source of our hope.

> Create in me a clean heart, O God,
>
> and put a new and right spirit within me.
>
> Do not cast me away from your presence,
>
> and do not take your holy spirit from me.
>
> Restore to me the joy of your salvation,
>
> and sustain in me a willing spirit. (Psalm 51:10-12)

I visited very different United Methodist churches in Florida on the Sunday mornings since I returned from the Special Session in St. Louis. They share in common excellent pastoral leadership. There was diversity of thought about the outcomes of the Special Session among a broad spectrum who spoke to me. And there was a real appreciation for the work, as imperfect and unfinished as it is.

What I discovered is what I should have known already. Social media is not the church. Political groups are not the church. Even petitions and plans are not the church.

The church is a living, breathing body. The church knows its sin well enough to confess it. The church knows its blessings well enough to thank God for them. The church sees beyond issues to people. The church does not have the luxury of excluding anyone.

I thank God for the local church and for pastors and leaders who sustain them. And mostly for the Lord who is lifted high in the midst of it all.

A month away from St. Louis, as the season of Lent began, I reflected on the outcome of the Special Session and what it meant for our denomination and the local churches that make it up.

I grieved the harm done to LGBTQ persons. The Council of Bishops expressed this also in a pastoral letter in December 2018.

I realized that the continuing work of justice in relation to the Special Session of the General Conference was in the hands of the General Commission of the General Conference—the executive committee of the Council of Bishops asked for an independent investigation into voting irregularities—and the Judicial Council, which would meet in a few weeks to determine the constitutionality of the actions of the General Conference.

I saw hope in the conversations that are happening across the church. Margaret Wheatley has noted that conversation is the currency of change. Some conversation is between centrists and progressives. Some conversation is between conservatives leaning in and conservatives leaning out. Some conversations are for the purpose of unity. Some conversations are for the purpose of division. More conversation is better than less conversation.

When persons are harmed, the responses are understandable. Some want to create distance. Some shut down. And some retaliate.

I continued to affirm, perhaps especially now, the resources contained in *The Anatomy of Peace* and the work the Commission on a Way Forward did on convicted humility.

One Sunday during this season I preached from the lectionary, 2 Corinthians 5. The Greek word for reconciliation is *katallage*. It is a word that appears only three times in the New Testament and was a word more commonly used in politics than in religion. It is a word about settling disputes.

God settled a dispute with us through the cross. And God now asks us to move toward, not away from each other, as we take up this ministry of reconciliation. It is linked, Paul will go on to say in the first verses of 2 Corinthians 6, to our salvation. Our salvation is not in fleeing from each other; the triune God did not flee from us. Our salvation is the way of the cross, our settling disputes with each other.

Finally, our hope is in the power and providence of God, in whose image we are all created, in whose church we joined through public promises, and into whose agenda we are invited.

That agenda is to resist the forces of evil, injustice, and oppression, and to turn to the crucified and risen Jesus, our judge and our hope. For the signs of hope, in conversations, in grace extended, and in justice sought, I gave thanks and continue to give thanks. God is not finished with us yet. And this is at the heart of what the Lenten season means to me.

# EDITORIAL IN THE
# *ORLANDO SENTINEL*

*The decisions of the 2019 General Conference in St. Louis had repercussions in local churches across the connection. In Florida, one of the communities most affected would be Orlando. I asked to contribute an editorial to the* Sentinel, *and they were open. I shared these words:*

In one of the world's best-known stories, a child who has wandered far from family and community and has been damaged by the world and harmed by his own decisions has an insight: "I can go home." The plot develops, and the characters emerge in the parable of the prodigal son in Luke's Gospel. And when the prodigal arrives, he is met by the welcoming embrace of a waiting parent.

The church and my own tradition, The United Methodist Church, is in a place of struggle. We want to welcome all people into communities of grace and love. We sing about this grace, we preach about this love. But despite our best efforts, we cannot translate all of this into our governance.

A part of the complexity is that The United Methodist Church is a denomination that is both global and democratic. The recent action of the Special Session of the General Conference retained traditional prohibitions against homosexuality, even as these are in tension with our social principles that speak of the sacred worth of all people. Many attempts to increase enforcement mechanisms about these prohibitions were found to be unconstitutional. A small number were included, and so the laws are somewhat stricter.

The result is disappointment and grief for many of our people in the

LGBTQ community and their vast allies. At our best, The United Methodist Church is an evangelical movement, which is about the motivation to share the love of God with others, with all. At our worst, we conform to cultural divisions, our mission becomes exclusive, and we do harm.

Seven years ago, I spoke one evening to a large gathering of LGBTQ persons and their allies at St. Luke's United Methodist Church. I had only recently arrived in Florida. And I wanted to convey a simple message: You are of sacred worth. You are not the problem. Your faith blesses us, your courage inspires us, your gifts strengthen us. Thank you for being in the church.

This remains true. The church is a gathering of imperfect people. We are all in some way on a journey home. We all long for welcome, acceptance, love. We struggle to hear the teaching of Jesus, and to become more like the waiting parent who welcomes all. This is both the mission of every local church, and the ongoing aspiration of twelve million people who gather under the cross and the flame that is The United Methodist Church.

*For me it was a pastoral word to a people who had been harmed. I received some feedback suggesting that I needed to step down from the role of bishop if I could not support the law of the church. I received some correspondence thanking me for leaning into the pain of the moment. There were parallel conversations with more traditional leaders, who felt marginalized by St. Louis. This was despite the outcome that had reinforced traditional convictions. And I would be in local churches over the next three Sundays, in Fort Myers, Jupiter, and Clearwater, preaching, listening, and leading through an emotionally difficult moment in the life of our denomination.*

# 2

# WEARINESS

I meet many, many people, especially leaders in the church who tell me that they are weary. Weary of division. Weary of the difficult nature of the work. Weary of the way being in leadership sometimes makes them a target. Weary of uncertainty.

I am with you in the weariness. And I have given some thought lately to what is at the core of this weariness, and what I am finding to be helpful. Not that I have discovered the secret of life here. But this way, I am at least managing to live with the condition of weariness.

1. I find it helpful simply to reflect on what is going on, as I teach and preach, and not to avoid it. I do some of this publicly, through writing and speaking. One occasion was a talk to our M-Lab group (a design thinking initiative), another a reflection with the UMC chancellors, another the opening sermon with the Council of Bishops. After the 2019 General Conference I gave a talk with our clergy session and the ordination sermon of the Florida Annual Conference. I find the process of trying to integrate what is happening with Scripture and tradition to be therapeutic to me. I hope it is helpful to others.

2. Searching not for balance, but for fun in the midst of it all. I would not describe my life as balanced. I imagine the same is true for you. Some days begin at 5:30 a.m.

(remember our church is present in many time zones across the world). But I have learned to schedule something fun in the midst of it all. During one particularly challenging week, I led a group of more than one hundred bishops who speak multiple languages, who have different visions of how the church can be faithful, and who imagine many different ways of using our time most wisely. We made it through. There will be some good fruit. And in those seven days I also saw the Cubs and Marlins at Wrigley Field, went on the architectural boat tour of Chicago, and visited Frank Lloyd Wright's home and studio, all with Pam. If you are weary, I recommend scheduling something fun. During the summer I spent a weekend with my sister and brother, as well as some quality time hanging out with a little girl named Paige (my granddaughter)!

3. Do constructive work even in the midst of the uncontrollable and uncertain. During the Way Forward process, I invested fifty days in meetings, with some of the most passionate leaders of our denomination, across the whole spectrum. And this was in addition to a full-time job. Many from the commission continue the work. Some of them do it full time. I do not. I am involved in the work, but have found that I need to focus also, in a both/and way, on work that is building something for the future. If I know the world would come to an end tomorrow, the wisdom has it, I would plant an apple tree today. We plant trees that will provide shade for those who will come after us. And so I led a retreat for those I would soon have the privilege of ordaining. I spoke to our large-church pastors and to our summer staff at Warren Willis Camp. We planned a fall M-Lab (design thinking training with

Jason and Hillary DeMeo) primarily for laity and also a
fall day apart for clergy on resilience.

4.  I know I write and read on digital media, but master-
    ing social media is simply a must. More often than not
    Facebook and Twitter add to the weariness. There are
    trolls. There is negativity. There are people who seem to
    be living the dream that we are not. There is misplaced
    anger. There is political despair, and lack of boundaries,
    and I could go on. And it does. So, I try to contribute
    to the social media but not become a monitor of it. It
    is like a stream that flows by. I love seeing the faces of
    friends and their lighter side. I rejoice when they rejoice
    and mourn when they mourn. But social media is not
    my church, political party, soap opera, or family. A prac-
    tice I recommend—try taking the first and last hours of
    your day without looking at an electronic device. Then
    increase that over time. There are many good alternatives.
    I have found that this helps to reduce the weariness.

5.  Lastly, I recognize that we are in an in-between time.
    There is no quick fix to our denominational divisions, or
    our national divisions for that matter. And if we divided
    in some way, or moved to another country, the basic
    human behaviors that have us hooked would simply fol-
    low us to wherever. Do you imagine that there is some
    pure form of church or politics that exists apart from the
    fallen and unredeemed human nature that is every one of
    us? We might as well work on it now, where we are.

So, if you are weary, you are awake, and you are living fully in the
moment. Ask someone you trust—a friend, maybe your spouse, or a
professional—to help you. We will all figure this out in a slightly different
way. This is what I am finding to be my way.

# 3

# UNITED METHODIST CHANCELLORS AND A QUAKER MEETING HOUSE

I traveled to Philadelphia to speak to the chancellors of our denomination (annual conference attorneys, traditionally those who give their counsel pro bono to the church), of The United Methodist Church. These are extraordinary women and men and this, their annual meeting, is usually scheduled following the Judicial Council.

I spoke about the sharp divisions of our church, the implications of our legislative and judicial processes the following winter and spring, the conversations happening in our church about the future and the bishops' role in these conversations, our need for practices of restorative rather than punitive justice, and the need to recover some of the work of the Commission on a Way Forward—a heart of peace rather than a heart of war, convicted humility, the importance of context, and the danger of a single story.

I also reflected on what it means to read the signs of the times—experiences of harm, fatigue, fragmentation, disconnect, sadness and anger, differentiation, resistance, and struggles with conscience—in light of the gospel.

Bishops do not write the laws of our church or vote on them. We are spiritual and administrative leaders. My first calling within that is to be a disciple of Jesus Christ. Jesus sought to fulfill the law through love of his neighbor, which was possible because of God's love for him. We simply must begin to understand the law in relation to love. This is the Bible.

I honor the work of the Judicial Council and the General Conference. Indeed, I am a part of this work. And yet what is true for us as individuals is true for our church. We will be saved, not by law, but by grace.

The next morning, I worshipped at the Arch Street Meeting House, a historic Friends church across the street from our hotel.

It was unprogrammed Quaker worship, which meant we were simply in silence for up to an hour. There were about fifty or so of us.

The first thirty-five minutes were silence. I prayed over a number of matters: our family, the clergy announcing new appointments today and their families and churches, the cabinet that had discerned these appointments.

I prayed for our church in the midst of profound divisions, for persons who have experienced deep harm, and for families who are themselves conflicted over where we are. I remembered that Edward Hicks, the painter of "The Peaceable Kingdom," often worshipped at this meeting house.

I prayed Scriptures that came to memory, especially the day's lectionary Gospel (John 20) about the announcement of peace that Jesus gives three times to the very people who have abandoned and denied him.

I prayed for the recent shooting victims in the San Diego area synagogue and visualized Jewish friends I had known across my life.

There was a deep silence in the room.

About thirty-five minutes into all of this a young woman stood and talked about intense pain in her neck and shoulders, and the relationship between mind and body and how silence and prayer had brought some relief. After a couple of minutes, she sat down.

A few minutes later I stood.

I told the story of my grandfather, who had been a Quaker. He was an engineering graduate of Georgia Tech and then of Vanderbilt. In World War II, influenced by reading the Gospels and Quaker pamphlets, he became a conscientious objector. During the war he did manual labor in the shipyards in Mobile.

His father wrote the head official of the Quaker church when my grandfather returned home to Columbus, Georgia, asking a simple question: "If there were no Quaker churches within distance of my son, could he still be a Quaker?" It was a carefully written, one-page letter.

He received a reply, also a page in length and also carefully written, from the Quaker official in Philadelphia. In essence, the answer was "Yes." My grandfather was a person of peace. He was a Quaker.

So, I shared this, in two to three minutes. I thanked them for their tradition and for their practice and told them I was trying to recover this in my own life. I did not say anything about my work, my role in The United Methodist Church, or the purpose for my being in their city.

The service ended a few minutes later. The people were very hospitable. A man named Andrew spoke with me. He inquired more about my grandfather, and then he said, very simply and clearly,

"You know, the postscript is that the letter is really written to you."

# 4

# THE WATER OF A WOMB

For many of us, and I am thinking perhaps of a favorite Bible you might have, for many of us the Bible just falls open to the Psalms. And one of my favorite Psalms is 139. I want to simply wander around in the space of that psalm, and I invite you to join me and consider as you read how God has worked in your own life.

> You formed me . . .
> It was you who formed my inward parts. You knit me
>     together my mother's womb. (v. 13)

My mother graduated from high school in June 1957, and I was born in August, two months later. I had always known that, but the meaning of it became stronger to me when she died in January, after an extended season of declining health. In divinity school I would learn about a concept, prevenient grace, and it expressed something that was a birthright gift for me. The sacrifice of a teenage girl, to give birth to me, how her life, her plans must have changed. I was able to thank her for all of this, how she bore the image of Christ as a young mother.

God forming my inward parts, knitting me together in my mother's womb.

My mother visited us in the summer of 2018, at Lake Junaluska. She loved it there, although she was not able to make the journey there very often. It was not the last time I saw her, but because of her health and my schedule and other circumstances, it was the last extended time we were able to really talk.

Our older daughter was baptized in the Memorial Chapel, also at Lake Junaluska. It was during the Western North Carolina Annual Conference. At the time I was assigned to four churches, and we did not want to choose between them, as a setting for the baptism, and we did not want to baptize her four times. It was around the time of my ordination as an elder and I did not want to be accused of violating the *Discipline* by rebaptizing someone!

Besides, this was home. And so, Bishop Bevel Jones said the words "Father, Son, and Holy Spirit" and placed water on her head. When I would visit him, he would ask about her for the rest of his life. How is that daughter of yours and Pam's that I baptized?

And in the summer of 2017, I was preaching at Long's Chapel, on the first Sunday in July, filling in for a friend who had become ill. After the service I received a call. Tomorrow your daughter will be induced, in Durham, to give birth. My wife was already there.

The end of my mother's life and the emergence of a granddaughter. I am somewhere in between all of that.

God is our creator, and the Scripture tells the stories of our lives. We emerge from the womb, a miracle, gasping for breath. We are surrounded by grace and providence. People have been planning for our arrival! We take our first steps and someone holds our hands. And then, sooner than we imagine, we take our last breaths, and, again, someone holds our hands.

Why is this psalm so powerful? Because it is about the intimacy of life, the most sacred moments along the way; and it reminds us that God is right there in the midst of it all.

You formed my inward parts. You knit me together in my mother's womb. In your book are written all of the days for me. I come to the end. I am with you.

# 5

# MOUNTAINS AND VALLEYS

The Bible reminds us that our lives are stories—I have sat on many porches and rocking chairs and told stories and listened to them—our lives are stories, but they are placed within an even greater story.

We are given the law. We somehow go beyond it. We fall short of it, every single one of us. But the Lawgiver does not give up on us.

God sends prophets—to remind us of who we are, created in God's image, of sacred worth, and that every person we will ever meet is of sacred worth.

I grew up in a Baptist church. It was located on Double Churches road. There were two churches on that road, and I attended one of them. The other was a primitive church, a hard-shell church. They worshipped every other Sunday and they did not believe in missionaries.

Missionaries only brought in the wrong people. Later when I would read the Gospels, I realized that was the point. We were all the wrong people, the gentiles. Jesus broke bread with us. They murmured. He told stories about lost sheep and lost coins and a lost child.

We were Baptist but not all of us. I would learn later that my grandfather was a Quaker. He was a conscientious objector in World War II. He read the plain teachings of the Gospels and tried to live by them. And he read the Pendle Hill pamphlets of Rufus Jones and Thomas Kelly and Douglas Steere. He was my mother's father.

We grew up. I met a beautiful woman from North Carolina and became a Methodist. Being a United Methodist, even with our struggles, has been a gift to me. It has been God's plan for me. All along the way God has had a purpose for me. Some of that has been clear as I was ordained and later consecrated as a bishop.

I came to annual conferences at Lake Junaluska for thirty years. Memorial services, ordination services, revival services. Reunions. I connected with friends through good times and bad times. Each year, we caught up on stories.

This has been a great year.

This has been the worst year of my life.

Annual conference at Lake Junaluska was a safe place to share those stories. And I now know what I never fully claimed, that God was in those stories. If I ascend to heaven, you are there. If I make my bed in the lowest place, Sheol, you are there.

God is everywhere. But God has always seemed especially close to me here. Where can I go from your spirit? Where can I flee from your presence? In the best and the worst of times, God was here. If I had ascended to heaven, if I had descended to the dead.

The Jesuits call this consolation and desolation. Consolation, when I have felt most alive. Desolation, when I have felt most lost. This was a place where you could come to terms with that. And the spiritual exercises that I remember James Fowler leading us through, twenty-five years ago, and connecting it all with Psalm 139, helped us pay attention to that.

The God who created us is in all of that. How do I relate to that kind of God?

## Search Me and Know My Heart

*Search me and know my heart.*
*Test me and know my thoughts. (v. 23)*

I remember how bad the 2012 General Conference was in Tampa, people doing political and legal harm to one another in the name of God. It is a quadrennial activity that we perpetuate and seemingly cannot escape. And then Pam and I came to the jurisdictional conference, to Stuart auditorium. And my vocational question was, "Okay Lord, do you really want me to serve as a bishop? Does the church really want me to serve as a bishop?"

And then Robert McMichael and Jarvis Wilson began to lead us in worship and praise. And we sang "The Blood Will Never Lose Its Power."

It reaches to the highest mountain

It reaches to the lowest valley.

And I knew it. Whatever would happen, it would be okay. If I ascend to the heavens, you are there. If I make my bed in Sheol, the lowest place, you are there.

Sometimes God says yes. Sometimes God says no. Could I be at peace with that, I wondered when we made the pilgrimage to St. Louis, for the Special Session of the General Conference. What would the church say?

In between all of that time Robert McMichael had died, way before his time, and Jarvis Wilson would later almost lose his life to COVID-19. But the words came back to me.

For some the 2019 General Conference was a high mountain. For others it was a low valley. Could I be at peace with that, trying to listen to and serve people in all of those places? Could I imagine that God was working in the midst of all of it?

Well, yes, God was and is in the midst of it all. Sometimes God says yes. Sometimes God says no.

And I reminded myself that my life was actually God's, and that the church is actually God's. What was God saying to us? What is God saying to us?

# 6

# SEARCH ME AND
# KNOW MY HEART

## THE GRAINS OF SAND

The height and depth and breadth of God is the mind of God that is so expansive. Can we really count the grains of sand on a beach? Do we really know the mind of God? This leads us to humility. In the Commission on a Way Forward we came to a term: convicted humility.

Psalm 139 comes along in the Scripture to orient us to who we are in relation to a God who is intimately involved with all of the details of our lives and yet whose works are beyond our imagination. And whose ways are not our ways.

We know this if we are honest. It is what we sing in our best hymns— we are lost in wonder, love, and praise. Lost in the vastness of it all. And to be lost is to be in need of orientation.

## ORIENTATION

My life has always been oriented to come to Lake Junaluska, especially in the summer. Growing up in the heat of south Georgia, and living now in the heat of Florida, there is of course a longing for the coolness of a breeze and the afternoon rain.

2016   2017   2018   2019   2020

But it goes beyond that.

God uses places, people, prayers, and the Scriptures to orient us, like a compass, to who God really is. God is our true north, our sacred compass.

The psalm recalibrates our minds and our bodies and our spirits, and this place allows us to walk beside still waters, to sit here and imagine that he will restore our souls.

We need all of this. Spoiler alert: All around us is polarized politics, a violent culture, severed relationships, the contested unity of the church, deep disagreements.

We need a true north, a reminder of a living God who searches us, knows us, tests us, undergirds us, and never leaves us alone, no matter the vista, whether it is highest mountain or the lowest valley.

Later the apostle Paul would write that nothing in life or in death will be able to separate us from the love of God.

## PRAYING OUR ANGER

And so, the psalmist says, "search me." Not search other people. Search me. Search me and know my mind, my heart—in other words, all of me.

And then a portion of the psalm that seems disjointed:

> Hatred, Loathing, Your enemies are my enemies, I hate
> them with perfect hatred! (v. 22)

If you live long enough, you are going to harm someone. Someone is going to harm you. Someone is going to harm someone you love. The church, Thomas Merton said, is like the resetting of a body of broken bones. If you live long enough, you are going to collect some enemies. And anger and hatred will become a part of your life.

If you have missed any of this, I can only say, as a lifelong Southerner, "Bless your heart!"

There is a portion of this psalm that is sometimes omitted when the church reads it. Our Jewish friends would never omit it, but we are prone to leave it out. I first began to pay attention to these verses through the commentary of Eugene Peterson. If I were writing the Bible, I would leave these verses out! Some of our hymnals, in the responsive readings of the Psalms, do just that. They skip from verse 18 to verse 23.

But I did not write the Bible. And these verses are in there.

It's pretty raw, and that's what anger is. We have to do something with our anger. Anger can be expressed as violence. I live in Florida, and in seven years we have witnessed the murder of Trayvon Martin in Sanford, the Pulse murders in Orlando, and the Parkland student shootings in Coral Springs.

Our anger can take the form of physical violence. Or we can express our anger through words. Remember our saying as children, "Sticks and stones may break my bones, but words will never hurt me!" Hang out on the internet for a while and you will witness violence.

And then we can turn inward with our violence, toward ourselves. We know that when this happens the result is depression.

What do we do with our anger? The psalmist teaches us to pray our anger. Remember, this is the God who knows us, just as we really are, rough edges and all, and sometimes a stew of anger and hatred. We take it to the Lord in prayer.

And then, we say again, to the Lord, "Search me. See if I am a part of the problem. I have my own suffering, but how can I learn about the suffering of someone else, how can I empathize with their suffering, how can I see that I may be complicit in their sufferings?"


## ORIENTATION, AGAIN

To be oriented is to listen to our lives, the real lives God gives us, not the fantasy lives we imagine. To be oriented is to come closer to a God who is intimately involved in the story of our lives, the best days of our lives, the worst days of our lives. To be oriented is to pray our anger and lay stretched out on an examination table before a God who knows everything there is to know about us.

And loves us more than we could imagine. And whose voice says, I was there, before it all began. And I will be there, at the end of it all. Nothing can separate you from my love.

# 7

# CONVICTED HUMILITY

"We begin from the recognition that our members hold a wide range of positions regarding same sex relations and operate out of sincerely held beliefs. They are convinced of the moral views they espouse, and seek to be faithful to what they see as the truth God calls the church to uphold. It remains the case that their views on this matter are distinctly different, and in some cases cannot be reconciled. We pray the exaggeration of our differences will not divide us. We also recognize and affirm that as United Methodists we hold in common many more fundamental theological commitments, commitments which bind us together despite our real differences. These also have implications for how we understand and express our disagreements, and for what we do about them.

"Therefore, we seek to advocate a stance we have called convicted humility. This is an attitude which combines honesty about the differing convictions which divide us with humility about the way in which each of our views may stand in need of corrections. It also involves humble repentance for all the ways in which we have spoken and acted as those seeking to win a fight rather than those called to discern the shape of faithfulness together. In that spirit, we wish to lift up the shared core commitments which define the Wesleyan movement, and ground our search for wisdom and holiness.

"We remain persuaded that the fruitfulness of the church and its witness to a fractured world are enhanced by our willingness to remain in relationship with those who share our fundamental commitments to scripture and our doctrinal standards, and yet whose views of faithfulness in this regard differ from our own." (From *Daily Christian Advocate*, p. 127; Final Report of the Commission on a Way Forward)

I n the fall of 2017, the Council of Bishops listened to the work of the Commission on a Way Forward, and a part of the feedback was that it needed to be more theological. The moderators were dividing up responsibilities, and I took on the response. I asked Bishop Scott Jones, who chaired Faith and Order, if we could pull together a very small group to work on a theological statement that could then come before the Council of Bishops and the Commission on a Way Forward.

We brought together Edgardo Colon-Emeric (of Duke) and Sondra Wheeler (of Wesley), both members of Faith and Order, and Bishop Greg Palmer, who served on the commission, and we met for twenty-four hours. Greg Jones of Duke was our gracious host.

Out of this group came the concept of "convicted humility." I continue to believe it is an extraordinarily helpful way of thinking and believing. It is Wesleyan, but more fundamentally it is what it means to submit ourselves to the Lordship of Jesus Christ in relation to members of his body, which is the church.

While the concept was not an influential value in the General Conference itself, it can continue to serve as a resource wherever two or three of us are gathered in Jesus's name. In the kingdom of God nothing is lost, including our need for convicted humility.

# 8

# CONFUSING TECHNICAL PROBLEMS WITH ADAPTIVE CHALLENGES

I can remember when the church saw the experience of divorce as a technical problem rather than an adaptive challenge. Technical problems are clear, widely known, and the norms of a community are able to solve them. The problem is solved by observing the rules. A person experiences a divorce and the church responds—he or she is no longer in leadership, and certainly no longer in a clergy role. This is the appropriate penalty.

Over time, the church began to see divorce not as a technical problem, but as an adaptive challenge. Adaptive challenges are not easily solved. They are complex, messy, and at times beyond our human capacity. Adaptive challenges can take years or even decades to resolve.

I have discovered that we can read the Bible in such a way that it treats what is actually an adaptive challenge as a technical problem.

We discovered, over time, that divorce and remarriage was an adaptive and not a technical matter. There were many reasons for divorce, among them abandonment and infidelity, abuse, immaturity, and incompatibility. Why did the church change its mind about divorce? Why did the church change its norms, values, and behaviors? Why did the church begin to listen to the experience within families and place that alongside the Scripture and tradition that had been taught? Why did the church begin to read the Bible in new ways?

2016    2017    2018    2019    2020

Has it not been true that the church over time adapted to the experience of divorce and remarriage in families and embraced their gifts? Has it not been true that the church, at our best, began to think less about who paid a penalty and more about how we were restored?

And has it not been true that the church has ceased to do harm to families who have experienced divorce, precisely by not treating their lives as if they are technical problems—ones that are outside the rules held by the community—and realizing that the solution is one we are in the process of resolving, in all of its complexity, together?

What does this experience in the church, over the past generation, teach us about how we read and interpret the Bible in light of other experiences of the people in our families and congregations?

We honor the Scripture. And we recognize our need to interpret Scripture with careful diagnosis and with convicted humility, precisely because we honor Scripture.

The biggest single failure of leadership, according to Ronald Heifetz of Harvard, is to treat an adaptive challenge like a technical problem.

# 9

# THE MEDIATION LED BY KENNETH FEINBERG

At the May 2019 meeting of the Council of Bishops, we gathered to share the emerging conversations we were having. Some were public, others were of a more private nature. The legislative decisions advanced in St. Louis were clearly not tenable for our denomination. Large newspaper advertisements were taken out in many newspapers across the United States, with the names of hundreds of laity and clergy. This witness would be translated in a few short weeks into the results of resolutions and elections across the church that rejected the General Conference legislation at the annual conference level.

A question for bishops was clear: Would we be on the sidelines, observing these processes; would we lead them; or would we accompany them?

One of strongest emergent voices was that of Bishop John Yambasu, of Sierra Leone. He spoke eloquently of the damage done to United Methodists on all sides by the called session of the General Conference, and he spoke of his own prayers to God for intervention. This would become translated into a desire to meet with leaders, first from the conservative stream of the church. In our executive committee meeting in July 2019, I spoke to John of my absolute respect for him, and of the need to hear differing voices. I also noted that many of the more centrist and progressive bishops in the United States led annual conferences that had deep missional partnerships, relationships of giving and receiving, with African central conferences. His own sense of all this had led him to have additional meetings with key leaders of the broader church. And again, I very much respected his role and right to convene conversations. I had the sense that God was using him to help us find a way beyond the way forward!

At the same time Tom Bickerton, a friend from our days at Duke Divinity School and the bishop of New York, would rekindle a lifelong friendship with Jeff Greenway, chair of the board of the Wesleyan Covenant Association. The two called ten of us together for twenty-four hours of prayer, honest conversation, meals, and Holy Communion. Among the bishops were John Schol, Tracy Smith Malone, Cynthia Fierro Harvey, Tom, and me.

In time, these conversations would lead some to the sense that we needed some kind of outside and objective guidance. A small group met, through connections with a mutual friend, with Kenneth Feinberg. Mr. Feinberg is perhaps the best-known mediator in the world. He has worked with survivors of 9/11, the Deepwater Horizon BP Environmental Disaster, the Boston Marathon and Virginia Tech shooting victims, and the compensation of the highest paid executives following the US economic crisis of 2008.

A person of devout Jewish faith, he agreed to work with us, and said, "I will do this, pro bono. You will not see so much as a receipt for a cup of coffee from me. This is in the public interest." Bishop Gregory Palmer would later comment, "It is telling when those outside our own village have more faith in us than we do in ourselves!"

Almost immediately, a group of bishops and global leaders began working toward a mediated resolution that would allow persons with significant differences to find a path of separation. We met in Washington, DC in donated law office space, with the additional guidance of Rick Godfrey and Wendy Bloom. We would work for six intense daylong meetings, face-to-face, with many meetings via teleconference in between. There was representation from all four continents with a UMC presence, differing theological perspectives, varied sexual orientations, and frankly contrasting visions of the church's future.

There were sixteen of us, and the work was highly confidential. We were not speaking for the church, but we would speak to the church, hopefully, with one voice and beyond our own silos. We were each encouraged to have a circle of counsel, a confidential group with which we spoke and tested ideas. Since the resolution would in time flow through the hands of the General Conference delegates, I selected the first four lay and clergy delegates of the Florida Conference: Molly McEntire, Alex Shanks, Derrick Scott, Cynthia Weems, Alice Williams, Brett Opalinski, Heather Pancoast, and Magrey deVega. I wanted to know that what we were negotiating at that table was consistent with their values.

The work was stressful, and at times I wondered if our differences were simply insurmountable. Mr. Feinberg was truly a gift. He could be humorous and very direct. He was an extraordinary listener and yet also clearly leading us toward an end result that would be substantive.

He impressed upon us the need to compromise. One of his colleagues, Rick Godfrey, noted more than once that we had the opportunity to write our own narrative, and if we did not, the public would write the narrative for us!

As I listened, I became convicted that this was especially true in regard to the potential onset of trials related to LGBTQ persons and ministry. On January 1, 2020, the effects of the Traditional Plan, approved in St. Louis, would be in place. The narrative would be one of harm done to LGBTQ pastors and church members, especially related to weddings, if they were placed on trial by the church. I was convinced that this would become the narrative and would overshadow any good work that we were doing.

I also became convinced that two matters were of greatest importance to pastors who were more traditional and conservative in their convictions—their local church property and their pension. I respected this.

So I began to wonder: Could these two become connected—a moratorium on LGBTQ trials and a relaxation of the trust clause? This was clearly compromise. And it was a way to do less harm to two significant constituencies in our church. Each would be a way of writing a new narrative. And each would be a way of reducing harm, avoiding legal trials in the church and in the courts.

It would be a start. As I learned in our reconciliation work in Belfast, Northern Ireland, with my friend Gary Mason, if you are going to have a peace process, you must first have a cease fire.

What if this could become the narrative for The United Methodist Church?

# 10

# SPEAKING AT CHURCH OF
# THE RESURRECTION

In my role as bishop I receive a steady stream of letters. The great majority of them express two distinct values, and they can be summarized as follows:

- I want the church to love all people.
- I want the church to teach the Word of God.

Most of us have come a long distance to be here and at some sacrifice. I have come to a clarity about my hopes and dreams for the next church.

- I want the church to love all people.
- I learned this from reading the Word of God.

I have no desire to distinguish between a church that loves all people and a love for the Word of God.

If you want to quote Leviticus, I can place that verse in the context of Jesus's Sermon on the Mount. If you want to quote Romans 1, I can place that verse in the context of Romans 2 and 3.

If you want to quote Jesus's teaching about marriage, we can place that in a broader context of what he was saying about divorce.

With eloquence we can quote Scripture to each other. Of course, I could do this without love. And where I have done this, I have failed. Paul warns me about this in 1 Corinthians 13. If I understand all mysteries, but do not have love, I gain nothing.

I have given my life to studying, teaching, and preaching the Word of God. Do I understand it perfectly? I do not. This is convicted humility, which was one of the gifts of the Commission on the Way Forward to the church.

God has more to teach me, and this is the work of the Holy Spirit (John 16). And the implication—we will change.

We resist change.

And yet, we do change.

Change comes, in my experience, when we look into the face of a child or grandchild or friend who is going through a struggle with gender identity or sexual orientation. Change comes when we confess that harm has been done to people we love, and that we, people formed by the Scriptures and the worship of the church, have been a part of that harm.

And change comes when we receive the extraordinary gifts of followers of Jesus who identify themselves as LGBTQIA.

Along the way, we change.

We begin to hope that justice is restorative.

We come to understand that grace is amazing.

We remember the good news, that love "bears all things, believes all things, hopes all things, endures all things" (1 Corinthians 13:7). We search for a doctrine that sounds more like our favorite hymn or praise song and less like an ever-expanding set of rules and regulations.

We know about change in our spiritual and theological tradition. Many of us are even acquainted with the Greek word for change (*metanoia*). Change comes when we repent. The problem with this is that we want the other person to repent!

Over my lifetime, I have been in a process of change. When you love people, they change you. And when you immerse yourselves in the Scriptures, over time, they change you.

Change can open us to extraordinary gifts. But change also comes with grief.

I have spoken to friends across the full theological spectrum, and there is a common experience of grief. This has been mine.

Two Ash Wednesdays ago in Florida was the horror of the Parkland shootings. This past Ash Wednesday was only days after St. Louis. It was a time to recognize my own limitations and finitude. Over the last year there had been the deaths of two close friends from divinity school, then the death of my mother, then my father.

And amidst all of this the death—for now—of a form of unity that would have given a greater role for conscience across our diverse church and a greater inclusion of all people, and the elimination of the incompatibility language.

As a pastor I have tried to give others permission to grieve. I've not always been so good at that myself. My life of privilege has in many ways been an ever-widening experience of opportunity and growth and possibility. I have been and remain surrounded by abundance in most every way. I can count these many blessings and name them one by one.

But limitations are real. The most significant limitation may be my lack of faith. All of this teaches me to return, again and again, to God, and the path God really wants for me. And I know that from the Scriptures.

The rabbis, drawing especially on Psalm 119, insisted that there is no distinction between loving God and loving the Word of God. The Word of God brings us into the presence of God. And the early church made yet another connection—I cannot love God, whom I have never seen, if I do not love my neighbor whom I have seen.

I am confident that, whatever is next, God will be with us.

God's Word is a lamp to our feet and a light to our path (Psalm 119:105).

The path for me is walking in a traditional faith toward an inclusive church. It involves the call to Abraham and Sarah (Genesis) to leave the familiar; the Spirit poured out on all flesh (Joel); the parables of Jesus, especially Luke 15 and Matthew 13; the temple as a house of prayer for all people (Mark 11); the Spirit poured out on all flesh again (Acts 2); the discernment to expand the mission rather than to constrict it (Acts 15); Paul's redefinition of law as love of neighbor (Galatians 5) and his setting aside ritual law in favor of what matters more, faith working through love (Galatians 5); and new creation (Galatians 6).

It includes Wesley's definition of holiness as being made perfect in love, the way we love God and our neighbor (Matthew 22). It is "The Scripture Way of Salvation" and "The Almost Christian" and "A Plain Account of Christian Perfection." It is the Eucharistic theology of John Wesley and the hymns of Charles Wesley, and, yes, the house church preaching of Susannah Wesley. It is "Love Divine, All Loves Excelling" and "Come Sinners to the Gospel Feast." It is "And Can It Be."

So free, so infinite is the grace of God.

A tradition must change, because along the way we sin. We segregate, we suffocate, we oppress, we exclude, we see through a mirror dimly. We are always being reformed.

I say *we*. I am under this judgment. I am in need of this repentance. I am only speaking for myself. And that is the testimony I share with you.

I cannot give up my generously orthodox faith. I want the church to teach the Word of God.

I cannot give up my hope for an inclusive church. I want the church to love all people.

Faithfulness is not standing in place. It is a path. We are walking in the light of God.

We are not there yet. But I have seen the emerging church, bold and faithful, free for joyful obedience. I see it in you.

It is . . .

A church that teaches the Word of God.

A church that loves all people.

# An Examen in the Wesleyan Tradition

*I began to work on this as a shared spiritual practice, one that is rooted in our tradition as followers of Jesus in the Wesleyan tradition. It is in the form of a guided meditation. I have offered it in a number of contexts, including the Florida Conference Table and with the Pre-Conference Briefing.*

## Grace

I begin today by claiming my identity as one who is created in the image of God.
I am fearfully and wonderfully made.
I am of sacred worth and am uniquely gifted.
When I come to myself—the truth of who I am—I experience blessing.

I reflect on those persons who have been a part of my life today,
who have seen this in me, who have encouraged me.
Have I really been attentive to them?
Have I fully accepted their gifts?

I stay with these encounters for a moment.
I see the faces of these persons and listen to their voices again.

## Repentance

Next, I see the moments of my day that I regret.
I rely upon the fruit of the Holy Spirit, especially love, peace, and patience,
for help in returning to these moments.
This is uncomfortable.
And yet repentance that is of God is a return to the love God wants for me.
It is the journey home.

For a moment, I consider the ways I am stuck, or lost.
Why do I resist change?
I ask for the courage to return to God.

## Confession

As I reflect on the day,
I ask God to reveal the harm that I have done to others
and the harm I have done to myself.
I make an honest assessment of my failures and mistakes.
Where I have not loved my neighbor as myself, I confess that I have sinned.

What is the sin that separates me from those closest to me?
How does arrogance, judgmentalism, ego, or privilege distort the way I
    see others?
How have I buried my birthright gifts and refused to enjoy and share them?

## Faith

I ask for the gift of God's healing and renewing grace.
I set aside my own claims of righteousness or merit.
In faith I say yes to Jesus Christ, who loves me and gave himself for me.
I place my trust in Jesus Christ alone for the gift of salvation.

And for a moment, I consider how I am actually living by faith.
Do I find it difficult to trust?

I return to the good news that I embraced when I first began to walk with
   Jesus.
I ask that God would empower me to live this day in faith.


# LOVE

God has created me.
God knows me.
God's sacrificial love in the crucified Jesus is for my salvation.
When I have received the gift of faith, I become a more loving person.
And when I have placed my faith and trust in Jesus Christ,
I become a part of his body, which is the church.

I boldly ask that I will be made perfect in love in this life—
that I will love God,
and love the people I encounter each day in God.

I ask that my love for God would grow as I read the Scriptures,
spend time in prayer, and receive Communion as often as possible.

I ask God to give me a greater love for others,
especially those to whom I have made promises and covenants,
and those with whom I have differences.

I ask God for the happiness that is taking the daily risk of living in grace,
practicing repentance and confession,
and growing in a faith that expresses itself through love.

Amen.

# 11

# Preaching and Breaking Bread Amidst Complaints

Immediately following the General Conference in February 2019, I received a complaint brought by one of our Florida Conference clergy against another, regarding a same-gender wedding.

We began to process the complaint, according to *The Book of Discipline*. While most clergy complaints are private, and there is an inherent dignity in this pattern, this particular complaint became public. Both parties were identified with broader movements in our church that have opposing visions and hopes for the future.

I met with them to work on a just resolution. Each had a support person present. I told them I saw them not as members of particular caucus or renewal groups but as members of our annual conference and actually pastors in the same district.

I have done a great deal of work on restorative justice, through the Harvard Program on Negotiation, ReThinking Conflict in Belfast, Northern Ireland, and in the mediation work of the Way Forward.

I am not naive about the complexities that lead to conflict or arrogant about my own skills. But I am always hopeful. And yet on this day we did not achieve a just resolution. We did share Communion together. They did agree to publicly pray for each other. And I decided that in the coming year I wanted to preach in each of their churches.

And so, within the next year I did. I preached at one of the churches, in Tampa on their 125th Anniversary and publicly thanked their pastor. I preached at the other pastor's church on Ash Wednesday and publicly prayed for him. I shared a meal with both of them on these occasions and met their families.

Finally, and as a signatory of the Mediated Protocol of Reconciliation and Grace, I decided to hold the complaint in abeyance. I had been a strong advocate for a moratorium on trials within the mediation.

Being in each church and with each pastor, I had a clear sense that a trial would not help either clergy or church. I claim this as my own discernment. It also helped me see these pastors in their contexts, which are very different. Context is difficult to honor when you are presiding at a General Conference or speaking to a Judicial Council. But when you are mingling with the members of a local church, it makes all the sense in the world.

It was an honor to preach the gospel at these two very different churches, and to break bread with these two very different pastors.

## 12

# THE ARRIVAL OF COVID-19

Community interventions are temporary and socially and economically costly. Individual actions are humble but powerful and permanent. Community interventions like event closures have an important role in limiting COVID transmission, but individual behavior changes are even more important.

*Professor Caitlin Rivers, John Hopkins University, Center*
*for Health Security*

We had heard intimations of the virus, but it happened quickly. The cancellation first of South by Southwest, then the NBA, then March Madness, then Spring Training, then the closure of Disney.

I began to change some of my own behaviors—I was to speak to the Northern Illinois Conference about Fresh Expressions, then a meeting in Nashville related to the General Conference agenda, and a meeting in DC related to the Protocol. These were all cancelled. Our appointive cabinet met virtually. This would, over a period of months, become the norm. I met briefly with some of our conference staff and assured them that we would prefer that they work remotely.

As a bishop and cabinet, we began to offer guidance to local churches in writing, by video, and in conversation, including support for not meeting for public worship. We have chosen to make those decisions with churches rather than mandate a practice. I have learned over time that if you treat people as mature adults, trust them and give specific guidance, they appreciate being a part of the decision. Most of our larger churches across Florida are not meeting in their buildings but offering online worship. I realize that there are other ways to go about this, and I absolutely respect this and the decisions leaders are making. We are also paying attention to service with the most vulnerable, partnerships in our communities, connection through technology, and financial sustainability

As president of the (global) UMC Council of Bishops, I requested the postponement of our General Conference, which at that time was six weeks away. The conference would include participants from four continents. That's a longer story. It is a complex decision, but really it was and is a very simple decision. As I was quoted in the UMNS story, I believed that this would save lives.

I confess that all of this led to the creation of a new mindset. I'm an active person, a social person, an extrovert. But those behaviors do harm in a season of the virus. It is counterintuitive, but we do love our neighbor (Matthew 22) by helping to flatten the curve.

Here was more personal motivation.

I'm just beyond sixty years of age. I'm very healthy, but I'm also in a health risk group. I want to be healthy for the long haul, for the hard work that will need to be done over the next few years. And flattening the curve is a way of keeping friends in health care professions safer. And I want to be a grandparent for a very long time (smile).

Over time I noticed behavioral changes:

I'm spending more time in conversation with family, friends, and coworkers.

I'm spending more time in intercession, gratitude, journaling, and reading Scripture.

I've been corresponding with UMC bishops outside the US who live in Europe, the Philippines, and Africa.

I'm spending a lot of time on conference calls, and I find that days are filling up with our staying in touch, planning and rescheduling, thinking together, communicating, and recording.

I take a walk each day, without getting within six feet of others. Getting outside for me became an imperative.

Over time I also began to reflect on individual differences, empathy, and intercession.

We do not all have the same contexts. Some are working in public ways—nurses, doctors, grocers, firefighters, police. Some have complex family responsibilities, such as loved ones with mental illness. Some are parents of children home from school. Some struggle with loss of income. Some have health challenges unrelated to the virus. Some are separated from family and friends.

This is about extending grace, bearing burdens, helping in ways that are practical and possible, and interceding. And, of course, all of this would stretch out longer than we would hope. We are extending grace. Most people are doing the best they can.

We attended to the practical: setting new dates for General and Jurisdictional Conferences, meeting with our treasurer Mickey Wilson to provide tangible help to every pastor and local church in the Florida Conference—our conference would fund half of the pension in the months of April, May, and June, representing an investment of $1 million, and freeing up resources to meet needs in local churches and in the lives of our members.

I recorded a sermon on "The Coronavirus and The Great Commandments of Jesus" for St. Luke's UMC in Orlando. Our appointive cabinet met (virtually) to reflect on our coaching calls with clergy in the districts. My guiding concern is to help people stay whole, to not be reactive, to take all of this one week at a time, and to position churches and leaders to be there when we would make it to the other side, which would turn out to be a much more extended journey than any of us imagined.

## SHELTERING IN PLACE

So, we began to shelter in place. I had decided to work from our home at Lake Junaluska, where my wife, Pam, was in the process of creating a beautiful garden, her therapy. I would walk and see the cross, daily, near the Lambuth Inn.

Here is what was happening for me: No traveling. No sports. No eating in restaurants. No face-to-face meetings or gatherings. All of this was quite disruptive.

This freed up time and I've found myself doing more of some other activities—I watched as little cable news as possible. In the spring I read through the Psalms and in the summer I read through the Gospels. I gave some Holy Week lectures on the cross (virtually) with Lovers Lane UMC in Dallas, taken from Galatians, Ephesians, and Philippians.

In prayer I returned to intercession, gratitude, and petition. Amidst the anxiety and in awareness and anticipation of the great suffering, I looked for signs of life, hope, and God in the midst of a changed spring. They were there.

I wrote an Easter letter to the (global) United Methodist Church, as president of the COB.

Audrey Warren and I sent in the final manuscript edits for a book on Fresh Expressions in relation to people and property. The last chapter is all about what we are learning about ministry when we do not have access to our buildings. We ended up needing to rewrite the last chapter.

I paid attention to financial giving in local churches, as the economy was devastated. What I saw was amazing. One large church had seen their giving increase and asked if it would be helpful to send in their apportionment for the remainder of the year. Another large church partnered with a smaller church near them. This was the 2 Corinthians 8 model.

I recorded an Easter Sermon in the Memorial Chapel at Lake Junaluska, where our daughter Liz had been baptized many years earlier. A number of Florida churches used it for Easter worship.

One of my favorite musicians, John Prine, died of COVID. Over the past year I had become obsessed with what would be his final album, *Three of Forgiveness*. He and I had been on a flight once, from Nashville to Tampa. I was so starstruck that I could only say, "I love your music." And he smiled in a self-deprecating way and said, "Thank you."

As the weeks passed there would be deep disparities in the rate of deaths among black and brown persons in our nation from COVID, and more hidden, among those living in rural areas.

And over time the pandemic would become a profoundly politically partisan reality. This is of course absurd, the point being we are all interconnected. The virus itself would teach us about what is real. And we would learn that many of those who were providing essential services lack access to health care. In David Brooks's words, this was like an X-ray of our culture, revealing what had been just beneath the surface, to some of us.

My friend and fellow bishop, Bill McAlilly, commented that our calling in this season was to provide emotional and spiritual care. He and I have both lived through disasters, he with Katrina in Mississippi and me with Irma in Florida. I think he is right.

Irma displaced 2.8 million people. There was a time of preparation, a time to endure the storm, a time to assess, and a time to respond, and that included longer term recovery work.

The COVID-19 pandemic is dissimilar in some ways. The time of preparation is extended and has economic and social consequences, because we anticipate an exponential impact (flattening the curve).

# 13

# EASTER AND BEYOND

The week following Easter of 2020 included a number of meetings, all of them virtual. Most pastors are trying to balance creativity, adaptation, and sustainability. Bishop Janice Huie spent some time with our appointive cabinet talking about "resilience." She had led retreats for us on this and it was a refresher we needed. It was very helpful.

I recorded a conversational sermon with Roy Terry, which was related to God's gift of creation on the 50th anniversary of Earth Day.

I began to see this as a time of paradox. A paradox is two truths side by side. It is a time of grief, anxiety, and loss. And it is a time of new creation, faith, and purpose. I find this psychologically and spiritually helpful. I find the Serenity Prayer to be helpful—acknowledging the things I can change, the things I cannot change. I find Jesus's teaching about living one day at a time in Matthew 6, a midrash of Exodus 16, to be helpful.

This is an extended season, over which we have little control, apart from our individual behaviors. We can continue to extend grace to each other. We can pray for each other.

We can see those whose sacrifices were actually contributing to our well-being all along in a new way. My wife, Pam, gave masks she had made to pharmacy assistants and women who deliver groceries and work in the post office.

We supported institutions and small businesses that were important to us, and we were determined not to take them for granted.

We recommitted ourselves to our local churches. And anticipated the day of rejoicing when we would be able to reassemble. And determined not to take that privilege for granted, if we had done so.

I made preparations for a (virtual) Council of Bishops meeting at the end of April, where I would give a presidential address with five brief themes:

1. Easter, the New Creation and the Pandemic: Returning to In Defense of Creation and God's Restored Creation
2. Vital Congregations, Fresh Expressions, and Why Every Church Will Soon Be a New Church (Relaunch)
3. A Traditional Faith and an Inclusive Church
4. Conferences, Councils, and the Connection: Living through Postponements
5. Adaptive Change and Staying Connected to Purpose

My language for our purpose:

> We live in the grace of God, through Jesus Christ. We are on a journey to holiness, which is loving God and loving our neighbor. We are in a connection with each other. We are not alone.

Our purpose shapes our practices during this time.

We pursue, perhaps more than ever, spiritual practices that are life-giving. We worship in online community. We help others in all the ways that we can.

We check in with each other. We call each other on the phone, we FaceTime, we write emails that express appreciation we have felt but perhaps not named. We know that we are not alone.

We held the meeting of the Council of Bishops, which was my final meeting to preside—I concluded my term as president on May 1, and we welcomed a new group of officers. The work was good. An astonishing feature of meeting virtually is that at one time there were twelve thousand watching the livestream. Five thousand people watched my presidential address. I am humbled by that.

I had asked the Council of Bishops and the Southeastern College of Bishops that I not be appointed to another leadership role in the denomination (to a board or agency, for example). I do believe in rhythms of engagement and detachment, and that feels right in this season. I have had four years of very intense engagement in almost every matter related to The UMC. At the same time, I have tried to give leadership with an extraordinary team to Florida. I believe other gifted people can serve.

There is still work to do, but in my mind the delegates to the postponed General Conference can and will do that work. More urgently, there is work to do in every community and congregation. I have never lost that focus, and now feel much more energy to devote to it.

## PREFERENCE, PURPOSE, AND PANDEMIC

In these weeks we are learning to distinguish between preference and purpose.

My preference would be to preach from a pulpit, to greet those present, to thank a local church for who they are in the community, to publicly praise the pastor, to name our connections. I have had the privilege of doing this in hundreds of churches in Florida over the past eight years. Afterward I would share a meal with the pastors and their families and get to know them better. It would usually include some really good seafood. All of that is my preference.

But right now, it is not about my preference.

It is about purpose.

Our purpose is to love God and our neighbor. Our purpose is to do no harm, to do all the good we can, and to stay in love with God. For United Methodists, that is our bedrock Scripture and tradition, the great commandment and the General Rules.

We are also people who love God with our minds, and that is reason. Faith seeks understanding. God created us in his image, and so we honor God by honoring life. It is no historical accident that Christians invented the first hospitals in the ancient world (see Kavin Rowe, *Christianity's Surprise*). Every church in which I served as a pastor included nurses, physicians, and health care professionals.

We connect all of this with our experience. God is in the suffering. God is in the lament. God is in the resistance to inequity. God is in the grief. God is in the loneliness. God is in the exile and wilderness. And God will be in the homecoming.

God will reassemble us when we know it is safe. This requires our trust, assurance, maturity, civility. It requires that we know how to think, as a church, and that we know how to distinguish between preference and purpose. And that we have the strength to lay aside our preferences for a season and allow God to teach us what God wants us to learn.

I was quoted in the *New York Times* about churches, worship, and the pandemic. And my words were directly in contrast to those of the president of the United States. This brought to me some criticism and some affirmation.

On Memorial Day weekend I gave thanks for those who gave their lives in service to our nation. At that time one hundred thousand had died from COVID-19. Soon, and my confession is that I had missed much of this, a new virus would emerge. And it would appropriately call for our response.

# 14

# I Can't Breathe: The Emergence of a Second Deadly Virus that Had Always Been There

Upon learning of the death of George Floyd, I would begin with prayer:

*New every morning is your love, great God of light, and all day long you are working for good in the world.*
*Today God is working for good through movements to dismantle racism.*
*Today God is working for good as scientists seek a vaccine.*
*Today God is working for good as ordinary people wear masks.*
*Today God is working for good through intercessory prayer.*
*Today God is working for good through faithful labor in all forms.*
*Today God is working for good in civil conversations across difference.*
*All day long, O God, you are working for good in the world. Let us see this, let us be encouraged in this, and give us the courage to be a part of your work in this world today.*
*Let this day be our offering to you.*
*And let this day contribute to your vision, in the words Jesus taught us to pray:*
*Your kingdom come, your will be done, on earth as it is in heaven.*
*Amen.*

2016    2017    2018    2019    2020

I began to call African-American leaders across our conference and to encourage cabinet members to do this work also. I then wrote a "Letter to My White Friends":

I cannot think of a single person with whom I do not want to be in friendship. Life has taught me that I have much to learn. In this life I have known some suffering but this pales alongside the privileges and benefits I've had.

What you do need to know about me is that I have seen racism in its visceral forms and in its sophisticated forms. I've been complicit in racism over my life.

What I've often felt but seldom said, is this:

It is a miracle that black people, brought as slaves to America by their Christian owners, did not turn in a wholesale way against Christianity.

That black people accepted the gospel can only be for one reason: that Jesus is real. It is supernatural grace. That blacks accepted the gospel is a miracle.

They have much to teach me (us). This has always been true.

But black people don't exist to be my teachers. They exist as creatures in God's image, and in Charleston, Brunswick, Minneapolis, Sanford, Long Island, Flint, and wherever we live, they want and deserve and dream about a full life of security and opportunity and flourishing.

Racism is antithetical to the gospel. Racism is heresy. Racism is sin.

Racism is going to be purged from us, in this life or the life to come.

I confess my sin in the things I have done and the things I have left undone.

I am grateful for the African-American leaders in The United Methodist Church who have been and are a part of my life.

This evening I pray for a church that sees you, hears you, and clearly lives in such a way that people say, "Oh, the Methodists," or "Oh, the Christians, they are the people who helped to end all of the ugly racism."

Not, "They passed by on the other side of the road."

None of this is worked out into a neat package. But right now, for Christians in the United States, this is the burning bush.

You'll notice I used a lot of language about "me" and not much about "you." I have my own work to do. This is a way of being honest about that. And it has to become a part of our friendship.

If I did not care, I would not be honest about all of this.

The work would be exhausting, but of course to say that as a white male only hints at the exhaustion of my black friends and colleagues. Still, it has been an exhausting week.

I had written several times about the death of George Floyd and reached out privately to a number of pastors and bishops. In a simple, imperfect way this is prophetic and priestly ministry, some of it public, some of it hidden. And, of course, it is a work in progress. I appreciate the words of my friend and colleague Gregory Palmer: we would need to move beyond crisis and catharsis and recognize that we are in this for the long haul.

I was asked to lead a time of intercessory prayer with the Upper Room. Over five thousand participated. Amazing. My relationship with the Upper Room has been long term—I have written for the daily devotional and for the *Disciplines*; I attended and served in the Walk to Emmaus; I trained in spiritual discernment with Danny Morris, who was a mentor; I have published two books with them; I loved the journal *Weavings* and mourn that it is no longer published; for years I spoke at the Prayer and Bible Conference and later SoulFeast; I have preached in their chapel.

I began to reread James Cone's *The Cross and the Lynching Tree*. This is a stunning and revelatory book, revealing a gap in my learning and a failure in my scriptural imagination.

I listened to Brene Brown's conversation with Ibram X. Kendi, author of *How to Be an Antiracist*. They are two courageous voices, and I am persuaded that Kendi is right. It was a God thing. I needed this conversation. A later learning would be that Kendi was a member of Mount Pleasant UMC in Gainesville, Florida, when he taught there at UF, that Dr. Geraldine McClellan had been his pastor, and that his parents remain members.

We are bitterly divided in an almost tribalistic way in the United States, and it has become clear to me that it is not about Republicans and Democrats. The partisanship is real. But in an extended season of economic disruption, a global health crisis, a season of racial injustice and justifiable protest, layered on our denominational journey related to inclusion and structure, these values are becoming clear to me. The values don't prevent me from being in relationship with anyone who reads this. They are in no particular order. In fact, they all hang together.

We needed/need to expand Medicaid. We need an economic safety net for those who do essential work. The Florida Conference has lobbied for this. These are the people who work seasonally in our state, who serve us in restaurants, clean hotel rooms, and make our economy function.

We need to wear masks. I wear a mask for you. You wear a mask for me. It is thinking more highly of the other person than myself. That is bedrock gospel.

Black lives matter. There is a historical continuity from slavery to lynching to segregation to mass incarceration. This is sustained by voter suppression. Visit any civil rights museum in the south—Birmingham, Atlanta, Montgomery, Memphis.

We can be a connection that has diversity from progressive to conservative members. Every church I ever served included this kind of spectrum. And we are a denomination that includes George W. Bush and Hillary Rodham Clinton.

As we learned in civil rights history, there are and always have been multiple theories for social change. Malcolm and Martin did not agree.

But the great story in the Bible, from Creation to new creation, is that every person is sacred, an image of God, worthy of redemption and healing, we all have sinned, and if we are the church of Jesus Christ we are one body in which all of the members fit together.

This is why black lives matter. In 2017 the Florida Conference passed a resolution affirming black lives matter, by a significant margin. On the floor Rev. Corey Jones spoke to this (white persons spoke as well). He said, and I am paraphrasing, "Every bone in your body matters. But if your ankle is broken, right now that is the bone that matters the most. This is where we are broken. This is why black lives matter."

One of the personal practices we are most in need of in this time is to lean into the "inescapable network of mutuality," in Dr. King's words. What does this mean in the present moment?

> The cross and the lynching tree.
>
> Your mask and my mask.
>
> I listen to you. You listen to me. I listen to you some more.
>
> I support your business. Your business honors my health.
>
> I vote. And I work toward laws that honor your right to
> vote.
>
> We read the Gospels together and learn from each other.
>
> When I reenter my church building, I do so with caution.
>
> And as a white person, I am not silent about racism, or my
> complicity in it.
>
> I extend grace to you. And you extend grace to me.

It could be that recognizing our connection, and in ways where we confront the real harm we have done, is one of the powerful "individual behavioral changes" of this season of two viruses.

# 15

# GOD WILL MAKE A WAY

I n preparation for the Fall, 2020 Council of Bishops meeting, I had read
Susan Beaumont's book *How to Lead When You Don't Know Where You're
Going*, which has the subtitle, *Leading in a Liminal Season*. Liminality is an
in-between place of ambiguity, wilderness, and confusion. It is a middle
stage of passage between the *known* of what has been and the *unknown* of
what is to be.

Beaumont would be a presenter in our meeting, the second virtual
meeting in a row. I was no longer the president or presider, and so this gave
me the capacity to be more present to what was going on. Cynthia Fierro
Harvey, our new COB president, led superbly.

As I listened to Susan Beaumont, I was struck by the profound wisdom of a single sentence. She said, "Most of us will end our careers before
the liminality is resolved."

I had written down this sentence. I underlined it. I highlighted it. And
the experiences of the past several years washed over me.

I had moderated a two-year process related to our global LGBTQ
conversation, the Commission on a Way Forward, that led to the General
Conference at St. Louis. I then served as president of the Council of Bishops for the next two years. This coincided with the Protocol on Grace and
Reconciliation through Separation, which we all signed, a symbol of some
kind of closure, and then the death of my mother.

And this was followed by a global pandemic, which would absolutely rearrange the schedule of the denomination, postponing all major

decisions, but more importantly it would take the lives of over two million souls. And then the visceral surfacing of racism, in the very public deaths of George Floyd, Breanna Taylor, Ahmaud Arbery, and concurrent visible expressions of white supremacy. And then the US presidential election, with a contested election, a contested transition of power, and an act of insurrection that led to violence and death. And all of this occurred alongside the decline of the church in many places.

> "Most of us will end our careers before the liminality is resolved."

I had seen myself often as a bridge figure on the way to the next church, but that statement really clarified it. As I write, I don't sense that I am at the end of active ministry; rather, I have a more settled acceptance that I am not in control of the events that are shaping the present season.

And this has a couple of meanings.

From one perspective, there is significant and real pain. My story here began with an excruciating injury, and a process of therapy that led to wholeness. All of the experiences I have just noted contain real harm to persons, most often those with less power and privilege. A mature faith requires that I stay with the grief and avoid a kind of sentimental denial.

From another perspective, a wilderness can be, in the language of the rabbis, "a school for the soul." I came to see that the LGBTQ conversation I might have avoided was in fact about grace and holiness. I came to see that leading a global body of leaders was about humility and listening. I came to see that not being able to enter our church buildings forced us to accelerate ways of reaching persons who would never enter those same buildings. I came to see more clearly my own racism, and that antiracism was an essential mark of discipleship in this moment. I struggled to integrate my spiritual life and my civic life and to find my public voice, especially in response to voter suppression and the good of democracy.

And through it all I returned to the concept of "convicted humility." My faith is stronger, even as the path is not of my own making. To be able

2016   2017   2018   2019   2020

to say that "God will make a way" is to admit some kind of peril or adversity. The way is not clear, at least to me, right now. There is no quick resolution of the resolution. And yet I am called to take the next faithful step, and in the movement, to claim that, through it all, God will make a way.

God will make a way.

# Acknowledgments

I am grateful to the laity and clergy of the Florida Annual Conference. Over nine years you have taught me about faith, courage, and compassion. My mistakes and blind spots would be most noticeable to you. I owe you a great deal. And here I am especially indebted to the members of the cabinet during these years.

I was blessed to come to know the members of the Commission on a Way Forward, and I give thanks to colleague moderators Sandra Steiner Ball and David Yemba.

The officers of the Council of Bishops were a constant source of strength and guidance, especially Bruce Ough, Marcus Matthews, Cynthia Fierro Harvey, and Tom Bickerton.

A few conversation partners made all the difference: Robert Schnase, Gregory Palmer, Gil Rendle, Janice Huie, Sue Haupert-Johnson, Bill McAlilly, John Yambasu, Grant Hagiya, Alex Shanks, Cynthia Weems, Greg Jones, Bob Tuttle, Audrey Warren, Candace Lewis, Will Willimon, Gary Mason, Alice Williams, Charlene Kammerer, and Lawrence McCleskey.

For friendship and meals along the way, I am grateful to Bill and Wanda Musgrave, Bill and Jacquie Wyman, Cam West, my sister Rita Bishop, and my brother Ben Carter. I hope the next years include more time for us to be together.

While my family is less central to this account of the last few years that appears in these pages, that is in part for their own space and privacy. In truth they were always there, at weddings, births and baptisms, holidays and homecomings, birthdays and anniversaries, at the beach and in the mountains. They were and are a reservoir of joy and stability, sanity and hope. For Pam, Liz, Abby, Allen, Paige, and Natalie, my deepest love and gratitude.

CPSIA information can be obtained
at www.ICGtesting.com
Printed in the USA
LVHW040042250321
682250LV00001BA/1